starting with rhyme

Nursery rhyme activities

for early years

Thérèse Finlay &
Jacquie Finlay

Authors
Thérèse Finlay and Jacquie Finlay

Editor
Jane Bishop

Assistant editor
Sally Gray

Series designer
Joy White

Designer
Heather C Hopkinson

Illustrations
Louise Gardner

Cover
Lynda Murray

Musical arrangements
Peter Morrell © 1997, Peter Morrell

Designed using Aldus Pagemaker
Processed by Scholastic Ltd, Leamington Spa

Published by Scholastic Ltd, Villiers House, Clarendon Avenue,
Leamington Spa, Warwickshire CV32 5PR

© 1997 Scholastic Ltd Text © 1997
2 3 4 5 6 7 8 9   7 8 9 0 1 2 3 4 5

British Library Cataloguing-in-Publication Data
A catalogue record for this book is available from the British Library.

ISBN 0-590-53718-0

The right of Thérèse Finlay and Jacquie Finlay to be identified as the Authors of this work has been asserted by them in accordance with the Copyright, Designs and Patents Act 1988.

All rights reserved. This book is sold subject to the condition that it shall not, by way of trade or otherwise, be lent, hired out or otherwise circulated without the publisher's prior consent in any form of binding or cover other than that in which it is published and without a similar condition, including this condition, being imposed upon the subsequent purchaser.

No part of this publication may be reproduced, stored in a retrieval system, or transmitted, in any form or by any means, electronic, mechanical, photocopying, recording or otherwise, without the prior permission of the publisher. This book remains copyright, although permission is granted to copy pages where indicated, for classroom distribution and use only in the school which has purchased the book, or by the teacher who has purchased this book and in accordance with the CLA licensing agreement. Photocopying permission is given for purchasers only and not for borrowers of books from any lending service.

Contents

chapter four

Mary, Mary quite contrary

chapter five

Humpty Dumpty

photocopiable activities

introduction

Children of all ages enjoy listening to and being involved in rhyme. Most children beginning nursery or playgroup for the first time will be familiar with at least some nursery rhymes. Those who aren't will soon become familiar with the constant repetition of rhymes provided at playgroup or nursery. They will quickly gain confidence and security by practising with the rest of the group.

Nursery rhymes are an invaluable resource within an early years setting and provide an ideal starting point for cross-curricular activities. They can be used to develop children's thinking and understanding by stimulating their imagination and firing their enthusiasm.

The range, repetitive language and rhythms of nursery rhymes provide a solid basis for encouraging early literacy skills. For this book we have selected five popular nursery rhymes to highlight the possibilities for early literacy, numeracy and other areas of the curriculum.

Getting ready for school

The activities in this book are designed for children who are working towards Key Stage 1 and tie in with the National Curriculum for Key Stage 1 and the Scottish National Guidelines 5–14. Each chapter provides: two activities to cover English, two for mathematics, and one each for science, design and technology, history, geography, art, music, PE and RE as well as two on display and finally a cookery activity. The activities also link with the *Desirable Outcomes for Children's Learning* for five-year-olds identified by the School Curriculum and Assessment Authority, providing a suitable curriculum for playgroups, pre-school groups and nurseries as well as for children in school reception classes.

Using this book

Each chapter is based on a specific rhyme, which the children will need to learn and practise. View each chapter as a 'theme' through which the children can develop their confidence and feel secure in their familiarity with the rhyme. The activities allow flexibility and can be used in any particular order to suit your needs or the children's interests.

The same format exists for each activity throughout the book, with a learning objective, group size, details of things you will need and any necessary preparation provided. The activity is then described and useful discussion areas are highlighted. Ways to support younger children and ideas to extend older children are also provided and further ideas for follow-up activities are also supplied.

At the end of the book there are ten photocopiable pages – two per chapter, each relating specifically to one of the main activities or the follow-up activities.

Displays

For each chapter two display ideas are provided. These should be central to the children's work, will provide a focal point and a chance for the children to contribute to the particular theme. The displays will stimulate plenty of opportunity for speaking and listening as the children reinforce completed work and add new dimensions as the theme progresses. The displays should also be a literary source providing purposeful questions, writing and reading activities alongside the children's own work.

Cookery

Each chapter contains a cookery activity related to the 'theme' which allows the children to engage in a practical, enjoyable task. Establish a regular hygiene routine before any cookery activity, making sure all children wear a protective apron and wash their hands thoroughly. Be sensitive to individual children's cultural or religious customs, and practices such as vegetarianism which will limit the consumption of some foods. Ensure that you are aware of any food allergies, intolerances or special dietary requirements and that all relevant information is documented for other staff.

Using adult helpers

Most of the activities work best in small groups, although adult helpers can be used to support children who may need extra help or those who are able to work more independently. During activities with large groups such as drama and PE it would be ideal for other adults to interact providing a role model.

The activities provide clear and concise instructions which you need to read and understand before the session, to help you deliver the activity with confidence.

Links with home

If possible, invite parents in to see and hear the work completed on a particular nursery rhyme. Encourage the children to recite the nursery rhyme at home with their parents and suggest that they tell their parents of activities which they have completed based on the rhyme. This will reinforce the work they have done and provide a further opportunity to develop their language skills. Parents are often astonished to see how much their children have gained from these experiences and how flexible nursery rhymes are.

chapter one
► introduction ◄

Old Mother Hubbard

Key D minor

Old Mo-ther Hub-bard she went to the cup——board to fetch her poor dog a bone. But

when she got there the cup-board was bare. *Spoken* Aaah and so the poor dog had none.

This rhyme is a good starting point for developing the children's sense of history. They will enjoy repeating this rhyme over and over again.

Considerations such as 'Why does Old Mother Hubbard keep the bones for the dog in the cupboard and not in the fridge?' provide an opportunity to discuss how we used to live before the invention of fridges. This can lead on to explaining what food people and animals ate and how food was preserved.

The children may be curious as to why there was no food in the cupboard, and how the cupboard could be filled. Most children enjoy shopping so encourage them to think about where their parents shop and how supermarkets are arranged into lots of different sections.

Tell the children how people used to shop before supermarkets; in small local shops that specialised in specific items.

An extended version of the rhyme exists which sends Old Mother Hubbard to different shops. From this the children could go on to discuss the geographical concept of how different buildings are used for a specific purpose.

As the rhyme includes Old Mother Hubbard's pet dog think about how to care for and look after pets. Ask children with pets at home to outline how they care for them and their particular needs. Stress that all animals are different so therefore have to be treated in a particular way.

The activities in this chapter are centred around food and animals and provide opportunities for the children to explore all areas of the curriculum.

Food, glorious food

Objective
English – to perform as a speaker and listener in a group situation.

Group size
Small groups.

What you need
Shopping bag and outdoor clothes for shopper, overalls for shop workers.

Preparation
Divide the group into three smaller groups to represent shoppers, shop workers (including till operator and shelf stacker) and family members. Discuss the tasks of each subgroup so that the children are clear about the different roles.

What to do
Explain that as Old Mother Hubbard needed to go shopping to fill her shelves, so the children are going to do the same.

Tell the children that each subgroup is going to have a particular task to do, in order that food can be bought and cooked. Brief each group:

Shoppers – the cupboards are empty and they need filling. Your task is to decide together what food is to be bought.

Shop workers – the shelves need stocking and customers need serving. Your job is to talk with your group and decide which food items need restocking, how to use the till and what to say to the customers.

Family members – you have returned home and want to know what you will have to eat and how long the meal will take to prepare. Have a chat around the dinner table.

Let the three groups work together to develop their role-play. Once they have had sufficient time to work together and develop their ideas the three groups can re-enact their whole section in sequence to show the order of events.

Discussion
As this is a discussion-based activity it is important to encourage the children to co-operate and work together in a small group.

Try to ensure that all the children are involved in the conversation.

Ask **shoppers**: What is your favourite food? Do you sell it in packets or tins? How much do you need to buy?

Ask **shop workers**: Which product is the most popular? Which foods would you stack next to each other? What buttons on the till do you need to press?

Ask **family members**: What would you like to eat? What have you done today? What are you going to do later?

For younger children
Choose one aspect of the role-play (shopper) and lead the conversation, giving helpful hints in order to move the children forward. Extend the activity further by using the role-play area to develop the idea after the initial input.

For older children
Encourage each group to make a written record of some aspect of their task. For example they could write shopping lists, complete stock sheets or make menus or price tags. The children may even enjoy writing down their dialogue and performing their scene from this.

Follow-up activities
▲ Develop simple scripts and use these within the role-play area; turn it into a recording or film studio!
▲ Introduce further characters and props to extend the dramatisation or create new scenes.
▲ Dramatise other familiar stories.

Going to the shops

Objective
English – to write for a purpose and recognise that writing takes different forms.

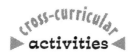

Group size
Small groups.

What you need
One sheet of A3 paper, a sheet of A4 paper for each child, pencils, crayons, coloured pencils, an empty box to represent the cupboard, one item of food.

Preparation
Turn the empty box into a cupboard shape with opening doors. Fold the A4 and A3 paper into the shape of a cupboard. Place an item of food inside the cardboard box 'cupboard'.

What to do
Place the cardboard 'cupboard' on the floor near to the children. Choose a child to represent Old Mother Hubbard and explain that she has fed the dog and now she is going to have her dinner. Send the child to open the cupboard for some food, when the child opens the cupboard she finds only one item of food. Explain that she must go shopping for some more food.

Ask the children in turn what they would like to buy from the shops. They can each reply using the phrase, 'Old Mother Hubbard buys some...'. Suggest that as there is too much shopping to remember, you need to record it. Introduce the large A3 'paper cupboard' and write or draw what the children would choose to buy on it.

Now give each child their own 'paper cupboards' (folded A4 sheets) to fill with shopping. Let them choose some items and ask them to draw a picture of each food item or write the words.

Discussion
Talk with the children about when they go shopping. Ask: who do you go with? Do you take a shopping list? Which shops do you go to? How do you get there? Are your cupboards empty or full?

For younger children
Scribe the words or encourage the children to create their own pictorial shopping list.

For older children
Encourage the children to write shopping lists either working independently or arranging the lists in alphabetical order. When reciting 'Old Mother Hubbard buys...' ask them to memorise and sequence the previous foods suggested by the other children (as in 'I went on holiday and I took...').

Follow-up activities
▲ Set up a shop in the role-play area.
▲ Make an alphabet book – think of a food for each letter.
▲ Make a shopping bag. Provide some coloured paper (wrapping paper, card) and materials for fasteners and handles (Sellotape, split pins, glue, stapler, ribbon, string) for the children to make their own bag.
▲ Play the memory game, 'I went shopping and I bought...'. Where each child has to add something new.

Little boxes, big boxes

Objective
Mathematics – to sort by a given criteria (shape or size).

Group size
Small groups.

What you need
Selection of packets, tins and cartons of food, picnic basket, rings to make sets in, paper and writing materials.

Preparation
Fill the picnic basket with the packets, tins and cartons of food. Make written and pictorial labels for each set (a set of cubes, cuboids, cylinders).

What to do
Place the picnic basket in front of the children. Explain that all the shopping is in the basket, but it needs to be sorted out, just like Old Mother Hubbard would, when she puts her shopping away in the cupboard. Open up the basket and take one item out at a time.

With each item let the children discuss the properties of the packet/container, considering the solid shapes and that these are made up of faces. How many are there? What shape are they?

Ask the children to place all similar containers/packets in a set ring and explain why they resemble each other. Present the labels to the children and ask them to match the labels to the correct set ring.

Once this is completed, place the items back in the picnic basket and choose a different criteria to sort them by. For example 'little and big', 'roll and don't roll'. After they have been sorted ask the children to guess why they have been grouped together in a set ring.

Discussion
Discuss in detail with the children the properties of two- and three-dimensional shapes (cube, cuboid, cylinder). Attempt to make comparisons between the two, asking: What flat shapes can you see on the cube?

How many faces has a cube got? How is the cuboid like the cube? Can the cylinder roll?

For younger children
Start by looking for two- and three-dimensional shapes in the environment. Limit the three-dimensional shapes to cuboids and cylinders. Provide different opportunities for the children to sort by 'like' shapes.

For older children
The children may enjoy sorting the shapes by their own criteria and asking their friends to guess the answer. Play a game where a child describes the properties of a food container, and the other children have to guess which is the correct container. Children could also design their own labels for different food containers.

Follow-up activities
▲ Show the children a selection of nets and investigate which shaped package it would assemble into.
▲ Invite the children to construct their own food packaging, using nets made out of card or a construction kit such as Clixi.
▲ Introduce further two- and three-dimensional shapes such as hexagon, pentagon, triangular prism and sphere.

Take your pick

Objective
Mathematics – to sort, match and group a selection of foods.

Group size
Small groups.

What you need
Paper plates, pictures of a variety of different foods (vegetables, meats, fruits, desserts), clear adhesive film, card, a copy of photocopiable page 87 for each child.

Preparation
Mount the pictures of food onto card and cover them with the clear adhesive film. Group the children on the floor and place the plates and covered food pictures in front of them.

What to do
Let the children take it in turns to describe a given food to the other children. In turn give each child a picture of a food item and ask them to describe the food to the other children, without actually saying what it is, or showing the picture. The other children must guess the food. If necessary demonstrate the first one for them, for example by describing a picture of peas – a small, round, green vegetable that tastes nice.

Next let the children sort the food onto the plates, choosing their own criteria such as all vegetables/all green foods/all round foods and so on.

Introduce the photocopiable sheet, naming all the foods on each shelf together with the children. Discuss which of the foods the children like to eat. Explain to the children that they have to match the shadows to the correct food on the shelves with a line.

Discussion
Suggest to the children that Old Mother Hubbard has decided to grow her own vegetables and talk about where vegetables and fruit come from. Discuss which grow on trees and which grow underground. Talk with the children about the various foods they eat at different meal times. Consider with the children how the different foods can be cooked.

For younger children
Simplify the activity by asking the children to use only colour and shape as a criteria to sort and describe the food. If necessary use silhouettes made from black paper to enable the children to experience matching the food on the photocopiable page in a more practical way.

For older children
Encourage the children to make some different silhouettes for their friends to match or guess.

Follow-up activities
▲ Set up a café in the role-play area and make your own play dough food to sell.
▲ Consider together which foods are healthy and unhealthy to eat.
▲ Cook different vegetables to try together.
▲ Write some healthy lunch menus.

Whose dinner is it?

Objective
Science – to find out about different living creatures and their eating habits.

Group size
Small groups.

What you need
Pictures of a selection of animals (ducks, birds, squirrels, lions, cows and lambs), a selection of pictures that these animals eat (worms, apples/nuts, pieces of meat, grass and milk), paper, writing materials, ribbons or laces, paper plates and Blu-Tack.

Preparation
Place the pictures of food on paper plates. Make labels for the food and animals. Place Blu-Tack at each end of the ribbons or laces.

What to do
Ask the children to look at each animal picture individually and encourage them to name them in turn; place the relevant label by each animal as it is named. Encourage the children to describe the animals in detail and highlight similarities and differences between them. Pay particular attention to the shapes of the animal's mouths.

Discuss whether these animals are living things and ask how we know this (they need food to survive, breathe and move).

Pass round the plates of food pictures for the children to examine and ask the children to describe them by texture, shape and so on. When each food is described and successfully named, label them appropriately.

Encourage the children to guess which plate of food each animal would like to eat and ask them why they think this. Use the ribbon/laces to link each animal to the correct plate of food.

Discussion
Talk about the animals' mouths describing the size and shape as well as the action used by the particular animals to feed.

Introduce some descriptive eating words such as chewing, gnawing, sucking, chomping and grinding.

For younger children
Focus the activity around two more familiar animals such as a cat and a dog. Follow this up with practical experiences using small world play, and a selection of pictures of food cut from magazines.

For older children
Provide the children with paper and drawing materials and ask them to predict the food which each animal may eat before the examples of food are revealed. Discuss in greater detail the criteria for living things: move, feed, grow, use senses and reproduce.

Follow-up activities
▲ Explore the eating patterns of various animals – predators, nocturnal animals and so on.
▲ Talk about and investigate animals' habitats.
▲ Tell the children animal stories and Aesop's tales such as *The Fox and the Stork*.

▶ activities ◀

I'm hungry!

Objective
Design and Technology – to use a variety of materials appropriately.

Group size
Small groups.

What you need
Modelling dough, paper, card, sponge, small paper plates, aprons, polystyrene pieces, writing and colouring materials, paint, tissue paper, PVA glue, scissors and modelling tools (cutters, rollers).

Preparation
Make modelling dough by placing two cups of self-raising flour, one cup of salt, four tablespoons of oil and two teaspoons of cream of tartar in a pan and stirring continually whilst boiling, until the mixture leaves the sides of the pan. Cover the work surface and display the range of materials in front of the children. Give each child a small paper plate and an apron.

What to do
Explain that 'Old Mother Hubbard' places the dog's food in a bowl, but we eat our food from a plate.

Discuss with the children what their favourite foods are. Ask them to describe what the foods look like, what shape they are and how many of each thing they have on their plates.

Explain to the children that they are going to make a plate of their favourite food using some of the resources available. Make up an example plate of food discussing with the children the appropriateness of the different materials for each food item. For example you can use scrunched tissue paper for peas, cut out pieces of sponge for chips and modelling dough for eggs and sausage.

Now let the children select their materials and make up their own chosen food items. Once they have finished their food items and stuck them onto the plate, encourage them to paint/colour the food appropriately.

To finish and to preserve the plates of food carefully apply a thin layer of varnish using PVA adhesive.

Discussion
Talk about the textures and how appropriate each of the materials are. Develop the children's vocabulary by using describing words such as spongy, springy, smooth and stretchy. As they work ask questions such as: how could you make the sausages bigger?

For younger children
Using modelling dough and experiencing the properties of the different materials is a valuable and necessary stage in the children's development. Encourage them to use rollers, cutters and shapes to improve their fine motor skills.

For older children
Challenge the older children to draft out their designs on pieces of paper highlighting the materials needed and what they expect the finished plate of food to look like. The children can choose what they view as the most appropriate design before making their plate of food. Once their plate of food is finished they should evaluate their product.

Follow-up activities
▲ Bake self-drying clay or modelling dough to make more durable plates of food.
▲ Design and make labels, menus and price tags for the plates of food.

How we used to cook

Objective
History – to recognise differences between now and the past.

Group size
Small groups.

What you need
Household equipment from 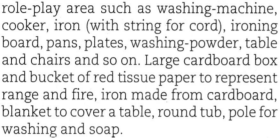 role-play area such as washing-machine, cooker, iron (with string for cord), ironing board, pans, plates, washing-powder, table and chairs and so on. Large cardboard box and bucket of red tissue paper to represent range and fire, iron made from cardboard, blanket to cover a table, round tub, pole for washing and soap.

Preparation
Make a kitchen range using a cardboard box and sticking black circles and rectangles on the top to represent hot plates, place the bucket of tissue in front of the box to represent the hot coals. Make an iron using cardboard, stand this next to the bucket. Use the tub and pole to represent a dolly peg and wash tub and place these next to the range. Arrange the modern kitchen placing the washing-machine, cooker, ironing board and iron on one side of the table and chairs and the kitchen from long ago on the other side of the table and chairs.

What to do
Discuss with the children the type of chores undertaken in our kitchens today. Ask each child in turn to perform one task in the 'modern kitchen'. Take each task in turn and encourage the child to describe how it is performed stressing factors such as, using electricity or gas, switching things on and turning them off.

Explain to the children this is how chores are performed now and ask them to guess how they were undertaken when Granny and Grandad were little – using the kitchen from 'long ago' to prompt them. When each task is suggested, ask the children to re-enact it in the kitchen from 'long ago'.

Help by describing the tasks in detail. For example say 'long ago there was no electricity or gas, so people had to use coals' (bucket of tissue, to be placed inside the cardboard box to act as fire); 'long ago to heat the iron people had to put it onto the range and they used a blanket on the table as an ironing board'; 'long ago people used a washing tub, dolly peg and soap to wash their clothes as they had no washing-machine'.

Draw the children's attention to the comparisons and differences as the modern day and old-fashioned tasks are performed in each kitchen.

Discussion
Discuss which kitchen would be the hardest/ easiest to work in and why. Talk about which kitchen the children would prefer to work in. Discuss any further aspects which can be compared such as lights/candles, toaster/toasting fork.

For younger children
Let the children role-play using the modern kitchen and the kitchen from long ago and highlight only one or two tasks for comparison.

For older children:
Record pictorially or write about the similarities and differences. Ask the children to write an account, 'A day in the life of Granny or Grandad'.

Follow-up activities
▲ Invite an older person to talk to the children about what things were like when they were growing up.
▲ Look at similarities and differences in other aspects of the home such as bathrooms.
▲ Compare and contrast how foods are prepared and stored now and long ago (fridge, deep freeze, larder, salt).

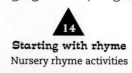

Stop and shop

Objective
Geography – to identify which food can be bought at which shop.

Group size
Small groups.

What you need
A variety of foods from 'fruit', 'cake' and 'sweet' shops, photocopiable sheet 88 one for each child, variety of writing and colouring materials, three shoe boxes labelled 'shop' to represent shops.

Preparation
Place the shop labels on the shoe boxes and put a mixture of fruit, sweets and cakes in each of the boxes.

What to do
Place the three boxes of food on the floor near to the children. Point out that someone has mixed the food up in the shops. Encourage the children to try and sort the food into the correct shops.

Choose one child to sort the food in front of the shops, and another to explain why the food is sorted in that way.

Ask the children which shops they would buy these items from. Then label the shops both pictorially and in writing, acting upon the children's advice. Now choose a child to place the items of food in the correct boxes using the labels as a guide.

Introduce the worksheet to the children, asking them to name the shops and the foods they could buy there. Ask them to match the foods to the correct shops and colour them in.

Discussion
Talk about different types of shops. Discuss what is sold in supermarkets. What type of foods are put together on the shelves? How big is your supermarket? What can you find in the fridges? Why do you have to queue up in supermarkets? Do you think smaller shops are better than supermarkets?

For younger children
Give younger children the opportunity to sort the foods practically into the shoe box 'shops'.

For older children
Ask older children to draw a picture of themselves by their favourite shop. Encourage them to label some of their favourite foods.

Follow-up activities
▲ Introduce another shop and discuss what food may be found there.
▲ Talk about where different foods come from, such as apples from trees.
▲ Consider what other local buildings are used for.

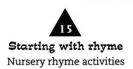

Mish mash print

Objective
Art – to use kitchen tools to explore pattern and make prints.

Group size
Small groups.

What you need
Paints in primary colours (red, blue and yellow), three shallow containers, paper, aprons, plastic table covering, whisks, kitchen cutters, fish slices, sieves and so on.

Preparation
Cover the work surface with plastic sheeting. Place paints in containers and lay out the kitchen gadgets on the table.

What to do
Carefully supervised, encourage the children to investigate the different kitchen gadgets paying particular attention to their purpose, size and shape. Encourage the children to predict what patterns each gadget will make on the paper when they print with them.

Let the children have access to paper and the paints and ask them to try printing using the kitchen gadgets. Initially ask them to stick to one colour to test out what kinds of marks they can make. They could go on to use all the colours and to make multiple prints of the patterns, either using a variety of gadgets or making a repeat pattern using just one in different colours.

Discussion
Talk about the similarities and differences between the gadgets. Consider how the patterns are made and relate them to the objects used. Which gadget has the smallest holes? Which gadget makes lines? Can you use two gadgets to make a recurring pattern? Why are all the prints different?

For younger children
Introduce printing to younger children starting with hand prints or fruit printing. This will help them to relate the finished print to the original object.

For older children
Encourage the children to use different colours to print with. Allow them to investigate what happens if two or three colours are mixed together.

Follow-up activities
▲ Devise a guessing game to find out which print goes with each gadget.
▲ Explore printing using other objects including small toys and a selection of found and natural objects.
▲ Use the prints as background or borders for displays.

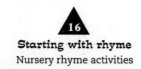

Woof, woof, miaow, miaow

Objective
Music – to listen for high/low, long/short and loud/quiet sounds.

Group size
Whole group.

What you need
Selection of animal pictures.

Preparation
If possible take the children to visit a pet shop or farm to observe animals in their own environment. Repeat the rhyme to the children and make up new verses introducing new animals.

What to do
Encourage the children to gently tap their knees, and discuss whether the sound made is loud or quiet. Next invite the children individually to experiment making other loud and quiet sounds.

Ask the children to make the sound of a mouse, and discuss whether a mouse's squeak is a high or low sound. Encourage the children to experiment making other high and low sounds.

Repeat this process each time using a different animal sound to emphasise the various aspects: long or short, high or low, loud or quiet.

Now introduce the animal pictures and discuss the various sounds made. For example show a picture of a cat, the child says 'miaow' and the other children then identify it as a high, long, quiet sound.

Once they have all had a go and discussed the different sounds choose a child to make a given animal sound using one of the above elements. For example ask a child to make an animal sound that is high ('tweet') or loud ('woof').

Discussion
Discuss any relationship that exists between the size of the animal and the noises made. Can an elephant make a high sound? Is a mouse sound long? Can you make a low sound? If you are little is your voice squeaky?

For younger children
Use a recording of actual animal sounds to help the children determine the differences between a loud and quiet sound or a high and low sound.

For older children
Develop the activity further by challenging the children to work in pairs and make an animal sound using two or three of the elements. For example 'moo' – a low, long and loud sound!

Follow-up activities
▲ Find out what sounds you can make using things in your group setting such as banging blocks.
▲ Sing 'How much is that doggy in the window?' changing the verses appropriately to include different animals.
▲ Use percussion instruments and listen for different elements of sound.

Slither, slide, crawl

Objective
PE – to travel in different ways and use different parts of the body.

Group size
Whole group.

What you need
Music of *Carnival of the animals* (Saint Saëns).

Preparation
Ensure the children are familiar with different animals and how they move. Begin by thinking about Mother Hubbard's dog. Ensure that the children understand that they must work in their own space. Listen to part of the taped music and discuss which animals are brought to mind. Make sure the children are in comfortable clothing and that they take off shoes and socks.

What to do
Warm-up
Encourage the children to move about the space using different parts of their body, in different directions – hopping, walking, crawling, sliding.

Introduction
Choose one child to decide upon an animal and invite the children to move like that particular animal in the available space. Pay close attention to whether the animal is big or small and moves fast or slow.

Repeat this activity choosing another animal that moves in a different way.

Main activity
Play the music and encourage the children to choose animals which move in a way appropriate

to the music, and to change as the music changes. Use demonstration to highlight good performances.

Cool down
Finish by letting the children move in the space using different movements as in the 'warm-up' section.

Discussion
Talk about the different actions and movements which animals make. Discuss the physical features which affect their movement (long arms, little feet, wings).

For younger children
Provide plenty of opportunities for the children to travel through the space using different parts of their body in as many ways as they can think of.

For older children
Let older children work in pairs, creating animal movements together. Provide opportunities for the children to mirror each other's animal movements.

Follow-up activities
▲ Try other pieces of music to move to such as *Peter and the wolf* (Serge Prokofiev).
  ▲ Use percussion instruments to create music to perform to.
    ▲ Sequence a set of animal movements together to make a dance.

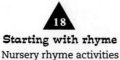

Would you like some?

Objective
RE – to be aware that sharing and caring are important qualities.

Group size
Small or large groups.

What you need
A comfortable place to sit, small sweets (one each), writing materials, one sheet of A3 paper, a sheet of A4 paper for each child,

Preparation
Cut each piece of A4 paper into the shape of a pair of hands. Cut the piece of A3 paper into a large pair of hands and label one hand 'caring' and one hand 'sharing'.

caring *sharing*

What to do
Begin this activity by choosing one child to share out some sweets amongst the other children. Discuss with the children how they used their hands to perform this task, in the same way as Old Mother Hubbard used her hands, to prepare and share her food with the dog.

Hands to represent Peacock's feathers.

Display the large pair of hands (A3 sheet) and ask the children to share their ideas on other tasks they can do with their hands. Develop the discussion into ways our hands can be used to help each other by sharing and caring.

Encourage the children in turn to describe a time when they have shared something with a friend. Record these ideas on the large 'sharing hand'. Repeat, this time discussing how they care for each other and animals. These contributions can be recorded in the same way on the 'caring hand'.

Once this is completed the children can each be given a pair or 'sharing' and 'caring' hands (cut from the A4 sheets). Ask them to record their own particular memory on their own 'hand' sheets.

Discussion
As this is a discussion-based activity the children should be encouraged to contribute when appropriate, take turns and respect each other's opinions.

For younger children
Invite them to draw a picture of a sharing time and ask an adult to scribe the event on their behalf.

For older children
Encourage the children to record their caring and sharing memories by writing on their 'hands' using sentences.

Follow-up activities
▲ Role-play some of the events, extracting feelings from the children.
▲ Create a peacock display from hand prints. Add a hand each time the children do something to share during the day.

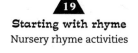

▲19
Starting with rhyme
Nursery rhyme activities

Let's go shopping

What you need
Coloured paints, white paper, coloured paper, shiny paper, tissue and crêpe paper, silver foil, card, shallow containers, sponges, wooden blocks, brushes, aprons, table covering, PVA glue, plastic lemonade bottles, Sellotape, Model Magic, art straws and coloured Cellophane.

Preparation
Cover the table. Cut out pieces of sponge. Cut some tops off plastic lemonade bottles, cover the rough edge with Sellotape to represent sweet containers. Make shallow boxes out of card to display the fruit. Make trays out of card by covering with silver foil. Ensure the materials are made available.

What to do
Organise groups of children to work on different sections of the finished display.
Pavements – print using a large wooden block and grey paint mixed with PVA glue.
Sky – print using sponges and pale blue paint to give an uneven effect.
Sun – tear strips of gold shiny paper to stick onto a circle and rectangles for the rays.
Canopies – use strips of crêpe stuck onto pieces of card, alternate two colours to form a canopy.
People – paint shoppers and shopkeepers.
Fruit – scrunch coloured tissue paper to make fruit shapes. Stick into boxes to be displayed in the 'window'.
Meat – make meat shapes from Model Magic (which can then be painted) or paint pieces of sponge to represent meat. Display them in the window on trays or hanging up.
Sweets – make lollipops out of art straws and tissue paper or card. Make sweets by twisting pieces of coloured Cellophane around sponge pieces. Make chocolate bars by wrapping silver foil around pieces of card. Make small sweets by scrunching up pieces of coloured tissue paper.

Use strips of paper to outline the shops, doors and windows. Print a title using sponge dipped in paint.

Discussion
Discuss what each shop would sell, how the food is weighed and packaged. Discuss how we know whether the shops are opened or closed. Talk about hygiene such as using tongs to pick up meat and washing fruit before we eat it.

Look in the cupboard

Labels on the illustration:
- net cap
- brown paint and p.v.a glue/wood grain effect.
- empty cupboard.
- wool
- Look in the cupboard
- are you hungry?
- Stuck on fabric
- wool or fur fabric
- old mother Hubbard went to the cupboard to fetch her poor doggy a bone....
- doggy
- But when she got there the cupboard was bare and so the poor doggy had none.
- paper bone

What you need

Coloured paints, chalk, PVA glue, paper, shiny paper, tissue paper, brushes, aprons, table covering, material, net, wool, fur fabric, old combs or nail brushes.

Preparation

Cover the tables and divide the display board in half.

What to do

Draw the outline of a cupboard on the left hand side of your display board. Ask the children to paint the cupboard using brown paint mixed with PVA glue. While the paint is still wet, drag a nail brush or comb through the paint to give the effect of wood grain. Stick shiny paper on the cupboard to represent handles.

Ask some children to draw a dog and stick on wool or fur fabric, to represent the fur. Make a bone shape out of paper to stick in his 'thought bubble'.

Make Old Mother Hubbard by drawing an old woman outline and use pieces of fabric for the dress and apron. Stick on wool for her hair and net for the mop cap. Gently chalk the face and use scrunched tissue paper for her features.

Repeat the above process, however the second cupboard should be left open, and the old woman and dog should look sad. The children could then paint an empty bowl for the dog

Attach a copy of the nursery rhyme to the display.

Discussion

Discuss with the children the different materials used.

Attempt to draw from the children reasons behind their choice of fabrics. Why use wool for the dog? Why have we made lines in the paint?

Shape biscuits

What you need

To make 12 biscuits you will need – 100g castor sugar, 150g margarine and 200g plain flour. Aprons, hand washing facilities, oven, covered work surface, bowl, sieve, scales, baking tray, shape cutters and a rolling pin.

Preparation

Ask the children to wash their hands using soap and to each put on an apron. Cover the work surface and place ingredients and equipment on the table. Switch on the oven to 180°c, and grease the baking tray. Discuss with the children the different shaped packets and tins Old Mother Hubbard would find in her cupboard.

What to do

Invite the children to help weigh the ingredients, sieve the flour and place all the ingredients in the bowl. Rub the fat into the flour and sugar and squeeze the mixture together into a ball. Roll out the mixture, and encourage each child in turn to cut out a shape, using the cutters. Place on a greased baking tray and cook in the oven for about 10-15 minutes.

When the biscuits have cooled enjoy them together!

Discussion

Talk about the appearance, smell and texture of the ingredients. Encourage the children to describe the differences that they see occurring in the ingredients, as they are mixed together. Discuss with the children the different shapes they have used and their properties.

chapter two

▶ introduction ◀

Hickory dickory dock

Key C

Hick - or - y Dick - or - y dock! The mouse___ ran up___ the clock. The

clock struck one, the mouse ran down. Hick - or - y Dick - or - y Dock!

'Hickory dickory dock' focuses on clocks and time and a good starting point is to investigate different types of clocks – their size, shape, features, textures, type and to sort and classify them in a variety of ways. The children may be interested to hear how clocks have developed and could even make a sand or candle clock.

The rhyme provides opportunities to consider what happens at different points throughout the day, establishing an early basis for telling the time. This can be extended into naming and identifying activities which the children take part in on different days of the week.

The rhyme features a mouse, providing an opportunity for the children to look at different animals and their habitats, ranging from wild animals to household pets. Children who have never seen a mouse move may not appreciate its speed and size; try to arrange for them to observe some mice and to copy some of their characteristics. They could even dramatise their own stories about a mouse or family of mice and all their escapades.

This nursery rhyme lends itself to developing a range of different language activities, as the children describe other animals and their features. The children could then try and develop this further into a game, whereby they describe an animal for the other children to name.

As you say the rhyme together, encourage the children to make the sound of a ticking clock by using a wood block. Suggest that a clash of cymbals could represent the clock striking one!

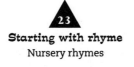

Where did he go?

Objective
English – to work in a group and communicate ideas in oral and written form.

Group size
Small groups.

What you need
White paper, sugar paper, pencils, colouring materials, felt-tipped pens, large sheet of card, enlarged copy of the nursery rhyme, picture of a mouse/toy mouse and a clock.

Preparation
Cut out and make a book in the shape of a clock for each child using white paper with a sugar paper cover. On the large sheet of card draw and cut out a clock to use as a visual aid. Display the nursery rhyme.

What to do
Show the children the clock and mouse and ask if these objects remind them of a nursery rhyme. Once they have guessed which rhyme you mean, recite 'Hickory dickory dock' together and discuss with the children where they think the mouse went and how he got there.

Ask the children to imagine they are a mouse and to think about the different places they could run to. Show the children the large segmented clock you have drawn and invite them to draw pictures in the segments, to show where the mouse may run to. Let the children suggest suitable places (shops, park and so on). Discuss the options they suggest and ask them whether the mouse would like the place, how long it would take and so on.

Finally ask the children to record in their own books the mouse's journeys; they can draw pictures or write their ideas.

Discussion
Ask the children: What type of clock was it? How did the mouse get inside? Is the clock big or little? How big was the mouse? How fast was the mouse? Where did the mouse live? What did the mouse like to do?

For younger children
Develop the children's positional language by asking them to place a mouse in different places on the large cardboard clock with the children's pictures on ('next to the roundabout', 'behind the shops' and so on). Encourage the children to act out the nursery rhyme.

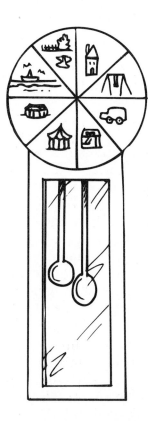

For older children
Encourage the children to create their own nursery rhyme book, starting with other rhyming phrases such as 'Yickerty, yackerty, yak'.
The children may also enjoy miming where the mouse went, asking the other children to guess.

Follow-up activities
▲ Create a word bank, displaying the words on mice shapes around a clock.
▲ Make a collection of different types of clocks; alarm clocks, stop watches and so on. Discuss what they are used for.

What's the time Mr Mouse?

Objective
English – to communicate and participate in a group as speakers and listeners.

Group size
Small groups.

What you need
Paper, writing materials, copy of the nursery rhyme, three coloured circles of card, rulers and Sellotape.

Preparation
Draw a grandfather clock onto a piece of paper and copy one for each child. Label each of the circles: morning, afternoon, evening and attach each circle to a ruler.

What to do
Choose three children to each hold one of the rulers with the circles attached. Invite another child to mime an activity which they complete during the day such as eating breakfast, getting washed, playing with friends, reading or going to bed.

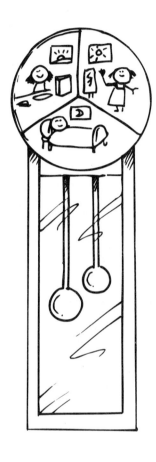

Let the other children guess what the child is acting out. Once someone has guessed ask the children which part of the day the activity normally takes place in. Once this has been identified ask the child holding the appropriate circle to lift it in the air. Repeat this game with different children three or four times.

Next, ask the children to place the activities in sequential order beginning with the things which are completed earliest in the day.

Introduce the picture of the grandfather clock to the children and ask them to record activities on the clock face in the order in which they happen in the day.

Discussion
Discuss with the children each of the activities in detail – how they are performed, with whom and when. Encourage the children to talk about why these activities take place at different times during the day. Ask, why do we sleep at night-time? What is your favourite time of the day? When do you get up? What time do you eat?

For younger children
Limit the number of activities and focus on morning and evening to begin with. Let the children draw pictures of activities related to these times of the day.

For older children
Use a clock to demonstrate the time that each activity took place during the day.

Introduce the term 'o' clock' and encourage the children to try and mime a suitable activity for each hour of the day.

Follow-up activities
▲ Sing 'Here we go round the mulberry bush', inserting the activities which the children have selected.
▲ Play a game using actions appropriate to the time shown on the clock. So, when the clock shows 8 o'clock the children stretch to wake up and so on.
▲ Make a daily timetable in the form of a clock and move a mouse to each activity as it occurs.

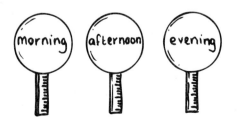

Tick 2, 3, Tock 2, 3

Objective
Mathematics – to sequence and recognise numbers up to ten.

Group size
Small or large groups.

What you need
Photocopiable page 89, one per child, writing and colouring materials, paw prints on card, picture of a mouse or a toy mouse.

Preparation
Cut out ten paw prints from card and label them with the numbers 1–10.

What to do
Practise counting up to ten with the children. Use different methods to count including clapping hands, tapping knees and nodding their heads.

Show the children the paw prints with the numbers on, and ask them whether they recognise the numbers. As each number is held up ask the children to clap that number of times.

Ask ten children to stand up and give them each a paw print to hold; ask them to name their numbers. Invite the other children to say if the children holding the numbers are in the correct order. If they are not ask them which number should come first, second, third and so on. Encourage the standing children to re-position themselves accordingly.

Place the paw prints in sequence on the floor as a number line. Choose a child to hold the mouse and make it jump from paw print to paw print, counting as it goes.

Introduce the photocopiable sheet to the children explaining that the mouse has to get to the clock by jumping on the footprints in the correct order. Encourage the children to make a path to the clock joining up the paw prints.

Discussion
Talk to the children about numbers which they see when they are out and about. Talk about odd and even numbers, numbers on doors, telephone numbers, their ages, how many days there are in each month, and how many months in the year.

For younger children
Restrict the activity to numbers up to 5. Invite the children to use the paw print number line as a resource and encourage them to move along the numbers in different ways such as hops and jumps.

For older children
Encourage the children to begin the number line at different places to start at 6 and count up to 10 for example. Extend the number line and invite the children to count up in 2s, 5s and 10s.

Follow-up activities
▲ Use the number line for practical addition: the mouse is on number 2 he jumps 3 prints what number is he on now?

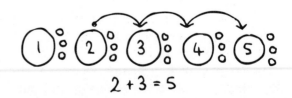

$$2 + 3 = 5$$

▲ Highlight odd and even numbers on a number line beyond ten.
▲ Create more dot-to-dot pictures for other children to complete.

Tick, tock, tick, tock

Objective
Mathematics – to sequence events and to develop the concept of time.

Group size
Small groups.

What you need
Photocopiable page 90 one per child, drawing and colouring materials, adhesive, paper, scissors, aprons and table covering.

Preparation
Cover the work surface. Cut pieces of paper into wide strips (approximately 40cm x 15cm).

What to do
Recite the nursery rhyme together and discuss with the children where the mouse went to at 1 o'clock. Ask them where they are at this time. Introduce the photocopiable sheet to the children, asking them to describe each picture in turn. Ask the children: What's happening on each picture? What time of day do you think it is? What makes you think this?

Discuss with the children what time they get up in the morning. Is it light or dark?

Encourage the children to think about which meal the girl is eating. Ask, what other meals do you eat during the day? What times do you eat these meals? Why are they called breakfast, lunch and tea.

Ask the children, what is the girl playing with? Is she at home or at playgroup? Do you like to play with a ball? Do you like to throw and catch or kick it? When do you play with a ball?

Explain to the children that the pictures are mixed up and need to be sorted into the right order. Discuss with them the correct order for the pictures and once they are clear which order they should take, they can colour the pictures in, cut them out and stick them in order onto a strip of paper.

Discussion
Discuss the days of the week and ask relevant questions such as: Can you name the days of the week? How many days are there in a week? What days are in the weekend? What type of things do you do at the weekend? Can you tell me something that happens to you each day?

For younger children
Provide plenty of opportunities for the children to discuss what they do and when during the day. Encourage the children to dramatise various activities for others to guess the time or the day the activity may take place.

For older children
Introduce children to the clock face concentrating on the o'clock and half-past and put an actual time to the events described. Use timers to measure the time taken to complete certain activities such as threading beads, building towers, or doing a jigsaw.

Follow-up activities
▲ Introduce the rhyme 'Monday's child' and ask the children to find out on what day of the week they were born; make a graph to show the days.
▲ Ask the children to record a day's events as a diary; extend this into a weekly diary.
▲ Make a graph of favourite meals.
▲ Make a group calendar showing special occasions that happen in a specific month such as Easter, Bonfire Night or Christmas.

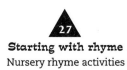

Bumpy, lumpy, soft

Objective
Science – to investigate differences between various materials.

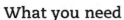

Group size
Small groups.

What you need
Paper, writing and colouring materials, set rings, a selection of textured resources (sand paper, tissue paper, stone, cotton wool, fruit, candles, wood, Cellophane, coloured foil, aluminium foil, sponge, foam, soft ball, plastic bag, book). Completed 'Touchy, feely clock' display as described in the display activity on page 36.

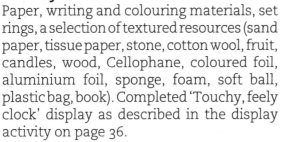

Preparation
Gather the children around the 'Hickory dickory dock display' (see page 36) and talk about the different textures they can see and feel on the clock. Arrange the selection of resources (see above) on the carpet in front of the children.

What to do
Choose an object and begin by using one word to describe it without actually naming the object. Pass it round to all the children in turn and ask each child to think of a different word/phrase to describe it. For example if you choose a candle the children may suggest – smooth, circles at each end, rolls, cold, hard, you light it and so on.

Encourage each child to then choose one object to describe in detail to the other children, using all their senses and appropriate language.

Next place all the objects in front of the children, and choose one child at a time to describe an object without touching or naming it. However, this time the other children have to guess the object being described.

Introduce the word 'opposite' to the children and explain its meaning, giving examples. Choose one child to pick an object and describe one of its properties. Ask another child to choose an object which has an opposite property. So if the first child chooses a wooden block, the second could choose a sponge.

Encourage the children to use the range of resources to sort and classify the items into a variety of sets. Let the children record the sets.

Discussion
As this is a discussion-based activity, provide opportunities for all the children to develop and extend their understanding and vocabulary. Consider the properties and textures of different clocks – what are they made of? Where do the different materials come from? What other things are made from these materials?

For younger children
Make a 'feely book' by sticking in different textured materials. Create simple sets, for example, all soft items or all hard.

For older children
Discuss the differences between natural and man-made materials, considering the properties of both. Look at the different processes used to extract natural materials such as paper from wood.

Follow-up activities
▲ Use a 'feely bag' to guess the different objects by touch.
▲ Test if it's possible to use other senses to guess/describe an object.
▲ Make models using different textured materials.

Open the door

Objective
Design and Technology – to use and investigate the properties of a range of materials.

Group size
Small groups.

What you need
A4 pieces of card, drawing and colouring materials, Sellotape, adhesive, paper-clips, split pins, ribbon, treasury tags, hole-punch, Blu-Tack, staples, scissors, table covering, aprons and some examples of flap books.

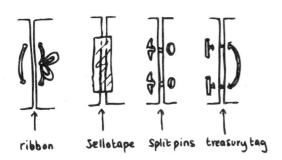

ribbon   Sellotape   Split pins   treasury tag

Preparation
Cover the work surface and make the resources accessible to the children.

What to do
Look with the children at different hinges – beginning by showing them some flap books. Discuss why these books have flaps, how they work and how they are attached.

Show the children a selection of resources, explaining that these can be used in different ways to make a hinge to go on a clock, like the one in the rhyme.

Demonstrate on a piece of A4 card how these resources can be used to make hinges. Use the correct names for the resources (ribbon, Sellotape, treasury tags) and discuss where they will put their door.

Let the children then draw and cut out a circle of card for a clock face which they can colour and complete including all the features. Attach the clock face to a piece of A4 card. Next let them cut out a piece of card as a door which they can attach to the

A4 card base using whichever method they choose as a hinge. Encourage the children to each decide upon the best hinge and the best point of attachment.

Complete the clocks by drawing a mouse and pendulum to fit behind the door.

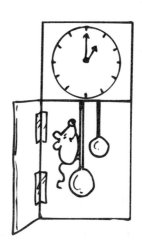

Discussion
Talk to the children about where they could find hinges, what they are made from and what purpose they serve. Discuss clocks that already have hinged doors and the workings contained behind them. The children could consider the purpose and differences in doors. Ask them: What are they made from? How do they open? What type of handles do they have? Do they lock? Can you see through them?

For younger children
Provide a pre-cut clock face and door for the children to attach. It would also help to limit the selection of resources from which the children can choose.

For older children
Make individual flap books, using hinges, to enhance the rhyme. Use the hinged flaps to hide the mouse in different pictures such as behind a tree, in the park and so on.

Follow-up activities
▲ Look at levers and how they are used in books. Try and include them in models which you make.
▲ Investigate how cogs work. Use construction kits to make your own model using a cog mechanism.

Playing in the past

Objective

History – to find out about chronology and to use words relating to the passing of time.

Group size
Small groups.

What you need
Selection of toys (suitable for babies, young children and older children), sack, paper, card, writing and drawing materials, bag, selection of baby equipment (clothes, toys, feeding bottles, food).

Preparation
Make labels saying 'Past', 'Present' and 'Future'. Place all the toys in a large sack. Place all the baby equipment in a large bag. Fold card into three sections, labelled 'Past', 'Present' and 'Future'.

What to do
Explain to the children that you have found a bag and you need their help to work out who it belongs to. Empty the bag containing the baby equipment out onto the floor and discuss each article.

Encourage the children to decide who the bag belongs to and why. Suggest to them that *they* would not use the things in the bag any more. Ask the children to talk about something they did as a baby that they don't do now.

Next, bring in the toy sack and choose a child to pick out a toy. Ask: Would you like to play with this toy? Help them to think about when they could play with it, introducing the words past, present and future. Set out the 'Past', 'Present' and 'Future' labels on the floor and ask the children to select a toy and place it in the correct set. Explain that you want to show whether they would have played with it as a baby, now or when they are older.

Finish by providing each child with a folded piece of card. Ask them to draw a toy from their own past, present and future in the boxes to create their own toy timeline.

Discussion
Talk with the children about what sort of nursery rhymes their parents might have sung. Ask do you think they would have sung 'Hickory dickory dock'? Are there any other nursery rhymes they might have sung? Compare today's toys with those parents and grandparents may have played with. Introduce phrases to reinforce the concept of time: in the olden days, a long time ago, now and when you grow up.

For younger children
Focus on the practical side of this activity and give younger children plenty of opportunity to sort a variety of toys and games into sets. Develop their historical language including vocabulary such as old/new/past/present and future.

For older children
Encourage the children to make timelines of events in their own lives, either using drawings or photographs. Let them try playing games which their parents or even grandparents played such as 'Oranges and Lemons', 'Whip and Top' and so on.

Follow-up activities
▲ Display other timelines showing photographs of the children throughout the year or to show the changes in seasons.
▲ Consider changes between past and present in a particular area such as school life or transport.

Starting with rhyme
Nursery rhyme activities

Around the clock

Objective
Geography – to find out about the local area and to introduce directional language.

Group size
Small groups.

What you need
Card, drawing/writing materials, glue, clear adhesive film, coloured counters and coloured mice.

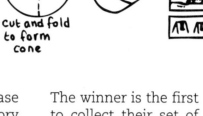

cut and fold to form cone

Preparation
On card draw and cut out a game base board in the shape of a 'Hickory dickory dock' clock divided into sections. Make small cards the same size as each section and different coloured mice.

What to do
Sing the rhyme together and talk about how the mouse ran 'up' and 'down' the clock. See if the children can name some other directions.

Discuss with the children features of the local environment, asking them to name places they like to visit.

Ask the children to draw and label two identical pictures of their favourite local place on separate pieces of card. Cover one set of pictures with clear adhesive film and stick the other set on the game board.

Discuss with the children how to show forwards and backwards, suggesting arrows if necessary. Let the children then decide which arrow and what number to place on a square. Cover the game board in film.

To play:
Place the board in front of the children. Ask each child to choose a coloured mouse and place a corresponding colour counter on each picture. Place the cards face down on the table. Choose one child to turn over a card. They must find the same picture on the board, move their mouse, collect a counter and follow the arrows. Put the card at the bottom of the pile.

Each child takes it in turn to turn over a card, move following the directions and collect the counters.

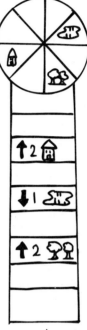

game board

The winner is the first to collect their set of counters. Throughout, reinforce the words 'up' and 'down' and remind them of the rhyme.

Discussion
Ask the children to talk about the things they like and dislike about the local area. Can they think of ways to make it better? Develop directional language by asking them to think about questions such as: What is next to the swings in the park?

For younger children
Children could use pictures of the local area to stimulate discussion and to familiarise them with the local area. Ask the children to direct each other around the room: go forwards two, backwards one.

For older children
Play a similar game but use further directions (sideways, left or right). Work in pairs to give and follow more sophisticated directions such as: forwards one, turn left, backwards three.

Follow-up activities
▲ Use a Roamer or programmable toy to follow directions.
▲ Make a set of instruction cards, using directions for the children to follow.

What colour's your mouse?

Objective
Art – to learn to mix primary coloured paints to create new colours.

Group size
Small groups.

What you need
The book *Mouse Paint* by Ellen Stoll Walsh (Orchard Books), paper, powder paint (yellow, red, blue), paint brushes, water, spatulas, aprons, table covering, containers, spoons, sponges, mixing palettes, elastic, card and finger paints.

holes for elastic

Preparation
Cut the card into five mouse faces and attach elastic sufficient to fit a child's wrist. Cover the work surface and put finger paints in containers on the table. Ask the children to put on aprons. Prepare the painting equipment by placing a spatula in each pot of powder paint, filling two containers with water, placing a spoon in each and dampening a sponge. (Ready mix paint can also be used. Place this in small containers.)

What to do
Read the book *Mouse Paint* to the children. This is a story about some mice who get paint on their feet, then dance in different coloured paint to mix a new colour. Choose one child to be the mouse by placing the mouse face on the child's wrist.

As you read the story emphasise the colours of the mice. When you reach the first colour mix in the book (a red mouse in a yellow puddle) ask the children to predict what they think will happen to the paint. Explain to the 'mouse' child that they are going to copy the mouse by jumping in the red paint and then dancing in the yellow; using fingers to represent the mouse's feet!

Let the child try this and check with the story that the same colour has been made. Repeat the above process, choosing a different child for each colour mix.

Once you have read through the whole story, place the equipment on the table and give each child a palette and a brush. Explain that they can mix their own paints by placing a spatula of powder paint on their palette and a spoonful of water, mixing it together with the brush.

Once the three primary colours have been mixed let the children create new colours, on their palettes or on paper.

Encourage the children to wash their equipment after they have finished painting.

Discussion
Talk about colours in the environment and how colours have associations. For example 'hot' or 'cold' colours and colours which represent danger. What colour are traffic lights? Why do you think red means stop? What colour do you think the mouse in 'Hickory dickory dock' would be?

For younger children
Before introducing the children to mixing powder paints provide plenty of opportunity for them to experiment using ready mixed finger paints. Make hand prints by painting each hand a different colour and rubbing them together to make a new colour.

For older children
Introduce black and white powder paint, discussing the effects when these are mixed with primary colours. Make colour shade charts, either checked, striped or spiral.

Follow-up activities
▲ Make camouflage pictures choosing one shade for the background and a shade darker or lighter for the object on top.
▲ Show some examples of the work of a colourful artist such as Jackson Pollock.

Clap your hands

Objective
Music – to perform simple rhythmic and melodic patterns by ear and from symbols.

Group size
Large groups.

What you need
A beater to act as a baton.

Preparation
Explain to the children that when the baton is held up they must stop immediately. Tell them to make sure they watch the baton at all times.

What to do
Begin by clapping a rhythm and encourage the children to copy. Start with a simple rhythm and then quickly progress to a more complex one. For example, start with one slow clap, through to one slow and two fast claps.

Once this has been mastered, explain to the children that they are going to clap out their own name. Clap out each child's name in turn and let the children copy. Following this, you should clap together the word 'hickory' – use the baton to show the children when to start and stop.

Split the group into two, one group still clapping 'hickory' and the other, 'dickory' – but only when the baton commands!

Now separate the children into three groups and ask each small group to clap 'hickory', 'dickory' or 'dock'. Again, the three groups must perform only when the baton signals to them.

Now invite the children to join you to clap out the whole nursery rhyme. Select a small number of children to tap on their knees the rhythm of 'tick tock'. Tell these children to continue the 'tick tock' rhythm while the rest of the group clap the rhythm of the whole nursery rhyme.

Discussion
Discuss with the children the difference between fast and slow claps. Talk about other ways to represent the rhythm, apart from clapping, such as using percussion instruments. What else can we tap to the rhythm? Can we wave our arms to the rhythm? Can we bang the drum fast or slow? Do you think the mouse runs fast or slow?

For younger children
Introduce the baton to the children and use this to direct them into clapping out a fast or slow rhythm. Initially hold the baton high for fast, lowering it for slow. Experiment with the baton, moving it quickly for a fast rhythm and slowly for slow clapping. Let the children take it in turns to conduct with the baton.

For older children
Use the nursery rhyme and the work completed on rhythms to create a round with the children. Introduce some percussion instruments to develop simple rhythmic patterns; try a tambourine or chime bars.

Follow-up activities
▲ Make a musical score by drawing a mouse, a pendulum clock and an alarm clock. Children can take turns to be the conductor and point to each of the pictures, while the rest of the class perform.
▲ Use musical instruments to make sound effects to compliment the nursery rhyme.
▲ Let children create their own rhythmic patterns and invite the other children to copy them.

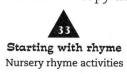

Stop and start

Objective
PE – to move in different ways and in different directions.

Group size
Large groups.

What you need
Wooden block, chime bar and beater, cassette recorder, taped clock sounds and a large space.

Preparation
Record a variety of clock chimes such as alarm clocks and cuckoo clocks, interspersed with chimes (perhaps using a chime bar). Reinforce the safety aspect of the children working in their own space. Let the children listen to part of the taped chimes before the activity begins.

What to do
Warm-up
Encourage the children to move about the space to the beat of the wood block in a variety of ways – jumping, skipping and running. Choose one child to hit the chime bar to make the other children stop. Repeat this several times, encouraging the children to use all the space and move in a different way each time.

Introduction
Ask the children how they can move about the space in different directions such as forwards, backwards and sideways. Repeat the warm-up encouraging the children to use different directions, stopping when the chime bar is struck.

Main activity
Introduce the prepared sound tape to the children, explaining that when they hear the chime they must stop and start again once the next clock sounds, travelling in a different direction each time.

Cool down
Arrange the children in a circle. When the clock starts, the children can slowly move forwards, when the clock chimes the children must stop and change direction – following your lead, either sideways or backwards.

Discussion
Discuss with the children how some movements are easier in certain directions, for example sliding forwards is easier than sliding backwards.

Talk about the parts of the body being used. Can all body parts be used to help movement? How many body parts touch the floor when you crawl? Which is the easiest way to move?

For younger children
Provide plenty of opportunities for younger children to stop on different commands, using their listening skills and sight, for example, clapping hands, tapping head or raising an arm.

For older children
Ask the children to devise simple sequences of movements, which they could then demonstrate to the rest of the group. Encourage them to follow pathways made by you, using skipping ropes or hoops.

Follow-up activities
▲ Create a game whereby the children change the way they move according to the number of chimes. So one chime means run, two chimes mean jump and so on.
▲ Play the game 'Grandmother's Footsteps' to reinforce stopping and starting when the 'Grandmother' turns around.
▲ Encourage the children to follow instructions on chime beats for stop, turn right, move forward, turn left and so on.

Don't run away

Objective
RE – to listen carefully, to respect each other's feelings and respond in a group situation.

Group size
Small groups.

What you need
Card, drawing and writing materials.

Preparation
Draw and cut out a large card mouse.

What to do
Ask the children how they think the mouse felt when the clock struck one. Do they think he was surprised or shocked for example? Ask the children if they can change their facial expressions to show different emotions for the other children to guess the feeling expressed. See if they can all make a face to show anger, shock, horror and happiness.

Choose one child to make an expression, and another to name it. Then ask this child to recall a time when they may have felt like this. Repeat this several times until lots of different feelings and emotions have been discussed. Scribe these feelings onto the large mouse shape along with drawings to depict the emotion.

The children could then discuss which of these emotions they like to feel, which they don't and why. Talk about how and what helps them to recover from these sad or nasty feelings.

Choose a child to retell an event, without naming which emotion they felt. See if the other children can guess the emotion.

Discussion
This is a discussion-based activity and you can encourage the children to participate as both speakers and listeners. Attempt to ensure all children have something to contribute but be sensitive to any children who are unwilling to disclose too much personal detail.

For younger children
Centre the discussion around events that have made the children happy or sad, encouraging them to talk about how they felt and why.

For older children
Encourage older children to write an account of a time when they felt a strong emotion. Consider with the children how others have strong emotions and that these should be respected, no matter how the individual copes with them.

Follow-up activities
▲ Make a 'Face book' with each page depicting a different feeling/emotion.
▲ Make a double-sided face attached to a ruler with two distinct expressions shown such as happy one side, sad the other or angry and calm.

Touchy, feely, clock

Group size
Small groups.

What you need
Sandpaper, felt, fabric, paper, card, coloured Cellophane, shiny paper, pipe cleaners, paint, chalk, PVA glue, crayons and felt-tipped pens, aprons, scissors, brushes, wool, string, polystyrene pieces, split pins, sponges, table covering and a large copy of the nursery rhyme.

Preparation
Cut card into circles, cut numbers 1–12 out of different textures and stick onto card. Cover the work surfaces.

What to do
Ask the children to work in groups on the following tasks:
Face of clock – prepare the background to the numbers by sponge-printing a large circle. Attach card with split pins to the centre of the face to make the clock hands.
Base of clock – draw a large grandfather clock shape. Use brown paint and PVA glue mixed together. Brush/comb through to create a wood effect.
Pendulum – make two contrasting pendulums, cover one in coloured foil and the other with matt paper, attach these to the clock base using split pins.
Mice – using the cut circles of card, cut each to the centre and fold to make a cone shape to form mice heads. Add mice features using pipe cleaners and pieces of fabric.
To assemble the display – glue the numbers onto the clock face, position the face onto the wall with the clock base underneath. Arrange the mice heads on and around the clock, and display a copy of the rhyme.

Discussion
Ask the children for their ideas to make the display better. What materials would they like to use? Invite them to think of ways to make the mouse run up the clock, or make the pendulums move. Ask questions about the material numbers on the clock. Which is the softest/hardest/fluffiest number?

Follow-up activities
▲ Make clock faces out of paper plates. Ask a child to set the clock at a certain time and then ask the others to mime an appropriate activity.
▲ Invent new things for the mouse to do at different times; 'the clock struck three and the mouse had tea'.

The clock struck one

hands made from card

Sponge painted circle

use combs to get wood grain effect

mice made from circles of card shaped into cones

Hickory dickory dock

Days of the week

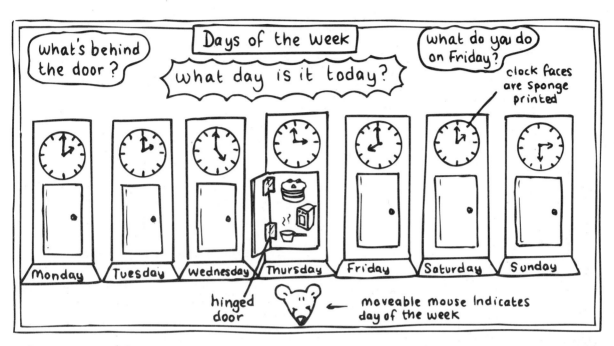

What you need
Paper, paint, PVA glue, paint brushes, sponges, felt-tipped pens, number sponges, stiff brush, Sellotape, stapler, card, table covering, split pins and shallow tubs of paint, combs.

Preparation
Mix the PVA glue with brown paint, cover the work surface and make the paint and sponges easily accessible.

What to do
To prepare the different parts of the display, encourage the children to take part in the following activities:
Clocks – ask the children to paint seven grandfather clocks using PVA glue and brown paint, which can be brushed/combed through to create a wood grain effect.
Faces – sponge-print the faces of each clock a different colour. When the faces are dry use the number sponges to print and complete the clock faces. Make clock hands from card and attach these with split pins.
Doors – cut, paint and stick a hinged card door on each of the clocks.

Daily activities – through discussion let the children choose and draw an activity for each day of the week to be stuck behind the hinged door.

To assemble the display – attach each clock face to a base and position the seven clocks on the display wall. Label the clocks with the days of the week. Use the display by opening the door on the appropriate day or attaching a movable mouse to the display to indicate the day of the week.

Discussion
Talk about the different activities completed during each day, and how these can be shown in pictures. Ask questions such as which is your favourite day? Which day don't you like and why? Which day do you go visiting and who do you visit?

Follow-up activities
▲ Make graphs to represent the children's favourite days of the week.
▲ Take photographs of activities on each day; compile them into a book.
▲ Make new pictures to hide behind the hinged doors.

White sugar mice

Group size
Small groups.

What you need
To make six mice you will need: 400g icing sugar, one egg white, 50g syrup, pink food colouring and a little cornflour. Aprons, hand washing facilities, covered work surface, bowl, string, silver balls, greaseproof paper and a sieve.

Preparation
Ask the children to wash their hands using soap, and to each put on an apron. Cover the work surface and place ingredients and equipment on the table.

What to do
Invite the children to help weigh the ingredients. Sieve 300g of icing sugar into the bowl. Add the egg white and syrup, mixing well. Slowly add the remaining icing sugar to the bowl.

Give each child a piece of the icing and encourage them to mould the mixture into a mouse shape using their hands. If necessary use the cornflour to dust the icing and prevent it from sticking to the children's hands.

Colour some remaining icing pink for the mouse's ears, inviting the children to mould it into ear shapes and attach them to the sugar mouse.

Show the children how to use a small piece of clean string to make a mouse's tail and to place small silver balls for their eyes.

Place the finished mice on a sheet of greaseproof paper and leave to set.

Discussion
Discuss the mice with the children. Compare their mice to the one who 'ran up the clock'. Ask: Which do you think is the bigger mouse? Which do you think had sharper teeth? Are the mice both the same colour? Do all mice have pink ears?

Follow-up activities
▲ Make different animal shapes from icing.
▲ Develop language skills by making different sized mice: large, larger, largest.
▲ Make a clock face out of icing and use coloured icing for the hands and numerals.

Jack and Jill

Key C

Jack and Jill went up the hill to fetch a pail of wa - ter.

Jack fell down and broke his crown and Jill came tum - bling af - ter.

**Then up Jack got and home did trot
As fast as he could caper;
And went to bed to mend his head
With vinegar and brown paper.**

Jack and Jill is a well-known nursery rhyme with which many children will be familiar. The tune shows variation in pitch and lends itself to highlighting dynamics. The children's enjoyment of performing the rhyme can be extended by introducing the use of percussion instruments to accompany the singing.

Percussion instruments could be phased in as the children's listening and performing skills develop. A xylophone could be used at the beginning and end to stress the movement of Jack and Jill up and down the hill. The sudden fall of Jack could be represented by clashing the cymbals, followed by the children saying, 'ow'. Finally a shaker could be used to portray them fetching the water.

Although they may be able to recite the words of the nursery rhyme, many children may be unsure of some of the vocabulary. Words such as pail, crown and caper may need to be discussed with the children. Explain that some words from the rhyme were words which were used more in the past, and have now been replaced by more modern ones.

This could lead on to discussing other aspects of the past, such as how people got their water from wells, and how wells worked. Talk about old-fashioned remedies, including 'vinegar and brown paper' as suggested in the rhyme and discuss the changes over time in hospitals and nurses.

As the nursery rhyme includes a variety of different actions such as tumbling and trotting, the children can consider other ways in which Jack and Jill might have moved, such as running, hopping, skipping, jumping, and so on. Extend this by considering where Jack and Jill travelled to and what they passed on the way – if this is represented in pictorial form it can provide a basis for simple mapping techniques.

Get better soon

Objective
English – to write for a specific purpose and to improve awareness of presentation.

Group size
Small groups.

What you need
Paper, scissors, writing and colouring materials, picture of Jack and Jill fallen at the bottom of the hill, a copy of the nursery rhyme and a selection of 'get well' cards.

Preparation
Cut paper in the shape of a bed for each child. Display picture and nursery rhyme in a prominent position.

What to do
Recite the nursery rhyme together and look at the picture of Jack and Jill. Talk about what happened to Jack, how he feels and where he will go now.

Ask the children to suggest how to make Jack feel better. They may suggest singing him a song, buying him a present or visiting him. Look at the selection of 'get well' cards and read the verses to the children. Discuss what message would be suitable for a card for Jack.

Show the children the cut-out bed shaped card and explain that they are going to write a card to send to Jack to cheer him up.

Give each child a card and ask them to draw a picture of Jack in bed, to decorate the card and to write a 'get well' message.

Discussion
Talk about where to send the letters. Can the children suggest an appropriate address? Discuss with the children what they think made Jack fall? What did he hurt? Did he break any bones? What treatment did he get?

For younger children
Provide a selection of prepared verses for the children to choose from and to stick inside their cards. Alternatively, scribe the children's own verses for them.

For older children
Discuss the rhyming words in the rhyme and encourage the children to apply these techniques to their own 'get well' verse.

Follow-up activities
▲ Provide opportunities to write in different forms such as thank-you cards, letters and birthday cards within a role-play setting.
▲ Hold a two way communication either with each other or with Jack from the nursery rhyme.
▲ Design and make other shaped 'get well' cards to send to Jack and Jill.
▲ Use photocopiable page 91; cut out and sequence the pictures and the words from the rhyme.

Who's who?

Objective
English – to participate in drama activities using appropriate language.

Group size
Small to large groups.

What you need
Bucket, selection of hats (police, fire-fighter's, nurse's, beret, cap, trilby, straw boater).

Preparation
Sit the children in a circle. Make the hats readily available.

What to do
Choose two children to act as Jack and Jill. The whole group can recite the nursery rhyme and the chosen children can perform the appropriate actions.

Introduce the selection of hats to the children and discuss with them who they think each hat belongs to. Ask them to imagine a situation where somebody wearing each hat meets Jack and Jill. Invite them to think what kind of conversation each person might have with Jack and Jill.

Choose two different children to be Jack and Jill and another child to pick a hat and take on the role of that character.

Explain to the children that while Jack and Jill 'walk up the hill', they meet a 'hatted' character to talk to. The rest of the group are to act as an audience and they can give suggestions if necessary. Repeat the process using different children to choose a hat and to act out the various parts.

Discussion
Encourage the children to think about developing Jack and Jill's conversation by relating it to their own experiences during the day. Ask: Who have you spoken to today? What did you say to them? What did they say to you?

For younger children
Limit the selection of hats available so the children can draw upon their own experiences.

For older children
Children could record various questions for each character, on hat shaped cards. Place these inside each hat for the character to ask Jack or Jill.

Follow-up activities
▲ Write simple scripts to perform.
▲ Dramatise Jack and Jill in different situations; at home, in hospital.
▲ Investigate one of the characters, find out what their job entails.

▲ **41**
Starting with rhyme
Nursery rhyme activities

What size are you?

Objective
Mathematics – to compare objects and to find out information from graphs.

Group size
Small groups.

What you need
Paper, scissors, string, ribbon, writing materials and adhesive.

Preparation
Place materials on a table allowing the children to easily access them.

from longest to shortest

longest ————————→ shortest

What to do
Recite the nursery rhyme together and discuss with the children how Jack and Jill got 'up the hill'. Choose two children to demonstrate how they travelled up the hill.

Ask the children whether the journey was long or short, and how could they find out. Guide the children into considering measuring with non-standard units (footsteps or strides). Provide plenty of opportunities for the children to use footsteps and strides to measure things in your room such as the length of a table or from one point to another.

Next, draw around the children's feet to determine the longest and shortest. Put the 'feet' in size order and make a display.

Talk to the children about how long the bandage for Jack's head would have to be. Ask the children to measure each other's head for a bandage using pieces of string/ribbon or strips of paper. Display the results.

Be very sensitive to individual children throughout this measuring exercise as some may not like being singled out for their personal attributes. Make it clear that everyone is different and that having small or big feet (for example) is acceptable.

Discussion
Ask the children to compare the size of their feet and their stride measuring. Discuss which is the longest, which is the shortest.

Look at the graphs and through questioning extract information. How many children have longer feet than child A? How many children have a smaller head than child B? Are there any children who have the same size head?

For younger children
Provide plenty of opportunity to measure practically using hands and feet. Let the children make hand and feet prints to use as a measuring tool.

For older children
Provide worksheets for the children to complete:
The table is _____ footsteps long.
The door is _____ hands wide.
Encourage the children to decide why they need standard measurements and introduce these.

Follow-up activities
▲ Consider how many footsteps there are in a stride.
▲ Count how many 'blocks' long the children's hand prints are.
▲ Find out if there is a relationship between the child's hands, stride and head measurements.
▲ Use photocopiable page 92 to develop comparative language. The children must draw a taller hill for Jack and Jill.
▲ Sing the song 'Heads, shoulders, knees and toes' together.

Fill the bucket

Objective
Mathematics – to use non-standard units to measure capacity.

Group size
Small groups of four to six children.

What you need
Water tray, coloured water, buckets and containers in a variety of sizes, aprons.

Preparation
Fill the water tray and colour the water (by swirling crêpe paper or food colouring around in the water; test for permanency). Place containers and buckets near by. Ask each child to put on an apron and position the children around the water tray.

What to do
Discuss with the children why Jack and Jill went up the hill and what they took with them. Ask the children what they would find at the top of the hill (a well) and what you get from a well (water).

Discuss with the children how wells work. Explain that an empty bucket goes down, and a bucket full of water comes back up. The water then needs to be transferred into something suitable for carrying it home.

Ask one child to choose a bucket to represent Jack's bucket, and ask them which container they would like to use to fill it with water. The children can estimate how many containers of water would be needed to fill the bucket and then test their predictions.

Repeat the process with different children using the different sized containers available. Encourage them to make their own conclusions about how many of each container would be needed to fill the bucket.

Discussion
Develop the children's language and understanding of how wells work, by using the appropriate language: lower the bucket, turn the handle and raise the bucket. Discuss how wells were used in the olden days, instead of taps.

Talk about the many different uses of water and consider how often during the day we use water.

For younger children
Provide plenty of opportunities for the children to play in the water tray using the containers to transfer water back and forth.

For older children
Make comparisons between the containers. Ask: Do the short fat ones hold more water than the tall thin ones?

Follow-up activities
▲ Using a set of containers investigate which holds the least, through to which holds the most.

▲ Complete the same activity using sand rather than water.

▲ Investigate water displacement by providing different sized containers full of sand to place in the water; discuss what happens to the water.

Roll up, roll up

Objective
Science – to identify that things can be moved by pushing or pulling.

Group size
Small groups.

What you need
A 'hill' (made from blocks and green card), two play figures to represent Jack and Jill, small play bucket, selection of vehicles and some string.

Preparation
Build a hill using blocks and green card and tie a piece of string to the bucket.

What to do
Recite the nursery rhyme together. Choose one child to take the Jack and Jill figures up to the top of the hill, and let them tumble down the other side. Discuss with the children how else Jack and Jill could have travelled up the hill (car, bike, bus).

Place a selection of vehicles near the bottom of the hill and ask a child to choose one for Jack and Jill to travel in. Once the child has moved the vehicle to the top of the hill ask them 'How did you make it move?' Repeat the same process for Jack and Jill to get down the hill – reinforcing the idea of pushing as a force.

Give the children the opportunity to experiment with the different vehicles using them up and down the hill and encouraging them to use appropriate language (faster, slower, push, pull, up, down).

Suggest that Jack and Jill have a car each but tell them that unfortunately Jack's car breaks down. Talk about how Jack and his car can reach the top of the hill. Suggest tying the two cars together and Jill pulling Jack's car up the hill – introducing the idea of pulling as a force.

Provide some practise of 'pulling' different things up the hill such as pulling up Jack's bucket with a piece of string.

Discussion
Talk about the vehicles used. Which was the fastest? Which was the slowest? Which goes the furthest? Which is the biggest? What toys do you have to push?

For younger children
Provide a selection of vehicles and three-dimensional shapes so the children can experiment practically, pushing and pulling.

For older children
Help the children to devise a method of recording their observations.

Follow-up activities
▲ Investigate what makes the best surface for the cars to travel on.
▲ Find out which car travels fastest when pushed down the hill.
▲ Display a large 'hill' picture and encourage the children to record the results of their investigations by drawing, cutting and sticking pictures of what they pushed and pulled up the hill on it.

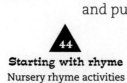

Round and round they go

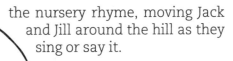

Objective
Design and Technology – to use simple mechanisms, joints, materials and components.

Group size
Small groups.

What you need
Card, split pins, wool, string, Sellotape, glue, stapler and staples, scissors and drawing materials.

Preparation
Cut the card into circles.

What to do
Explain to the children they are going to think about how and where Jack and Jill travelled and to think about the places and animals they may have passed on the way up the hill to the well.

Supply each child with a circle of card and encourage them to draw the well and some other things which they think Jack and Jill could have passed on the way (rabbit, lake, birds). This circle represents the hill.

On another piece of card ask the children to draw Jack and Jill. Discuss how they could be attached to allow them to move around the hill.

Demonstrate and describe how the various materials could be used and suggest the best way of attaching Jack and Jill to the hill circle (split pins through the middle).

Once the circle is completed with Jack and Jill fixed on, the children could recite the nursery rhyme, moving Jack and Jill around the hill as they sing or say it.

Discussion
Ask the children: Which is the best way of attaching Jack and Jill and why? Why does it move with split pins, but not Sellotape or staples? Develop the children's language (rotate, turn, moving, extend).

For younger children
Pre-cut Jack and Jill card shapes for the children to colour in and attach.

For older children
Attach the animals and well to the 'hill' with split pins to enable them to move independently too.

Follow-up activities
▲ Make a well out of card and use string to create a pulley for the bucket.
▲ Make figures of Jack and Jill, join their arms and legs with split pins and attach wool to joints allowing the arms and legs to move together.
▲ Make pictures of Jack and Jill moving along a road.

Ooh aah it hurts

Objective

History – to learn some stories and events from the past and to use artefacts.

Group size
Small groups.

What you need
Bandages, old-fashioned candle holder and candle, selection of hospital objects (nurse's apron, bag with a red cross, nurse's hat), large sheets of paper and writing materials.

Preparation
Place the artefacts in an accessible position for the children.

What to do
Discuss with the children how badly hurt Jack was when he fell down the hill and who could have helped him. Encourage the children to think of an alternative to Jill helping (doctors, nurses). Lead on to a discussion about hospitals and ask the children if they have been to hospital and if they would like to tell you all about it.

Explain to the children that you would like them to make a pictorial list of people and objects found in the hospital. Say that you will write their ideas down if necessary.

Show the children the collection of artefacts and ask if they could be used in hospital. As you show the candle explain to the children that a famous nurse who lived a long time ago used a candle when she went around looking at her patients. Explain that people called her 'The lady of the lamp'. Tell the children the story of Florence Nightingale, highlighting the reason behind her name.

Tell the children the story using the following key points:
• She was from a rich family.
• Although she wanted to be a nurse, her family said, 'no'.
• She wrote to the government to ask them if she could help.
• Eventually she was allowed to go and help the injured in the war.
• She looked after injured soldiers and carried a lamp with her.

Repeat the story with the children acting out the parts of Florence Nightingale and the injured soldiers she tended to.

Discussion
Discuss with the children the different conditions which nurses work in. Do all nurses work during the day? When do nurses sleep? What kinds of jobs do nurses do? What are the differences between nurses and doctors? Positively discriminate so that the children understand that men can be nurses, and women, doctors.

For younger children
Set up a role-play area as a hospital with plasters and bandages. Develop the children's language skills by introducing relevant vocabulary and encourage them to use the dolls and teddies as their patients.

For older children
Make lists of differences between now and then to include factors such as electricity, new machinery, computers, beds, candles and so on.

Follow-up activities
▲ Consider the lives of other famous nurses and doctors such as Mary Seacole.
▲ Discuss the problems encountered in hospital long ago such as medication being limited and the greater chance of disease.
▲ Look at other people in the community (police for example) and how their roles have changed.

Show me the way!

Objective
Geography – to develop geographical language and use pictures/symbols to make maps.

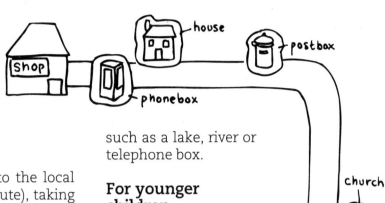

Group size
Small groups.

What you need
Paper, drawing and writing materials, camera and film.

Preparation
Take the children on a walk to the local shops (or similar short local route), taking three or four photographs of specific buildings or places on the way. Arrange the photographs into a simple map of the route to the shop.

What to do
Discuss with the children how they would direct a friend to the local shop. Encourage them to think of and name the various buildings or places they pass on the way.

Show the children the map you have previously made with the photographs from their walk. Encourage them to follow the route with their finger.

Ask the children to imagine that Jack and Jill have been invited for tea, but they need a map to get to you. Introduce geographical language by discussing possible things to go on their map, using the words: roads, crossroads, pathways, hills and rivers.

Help them to draw their maps, encouraging them to represent the features appropriately. Now let them try to draw a map to help Jack and Jill go from their house to the hill.

Discussion
Talk about moveable and non-moveable landmarks with the children. Which are the most reliable and why? Explain that describing walking past the river, as a landmark is more reliable than describing walking past a red car. Discuss the different ways to represent geographical features

such as a lake, river or telephone box.

For younger children
Provide the children with a pre-drawn sheet featuring a hill/well at one side and a house on the other with an interlinking road. The children can draw in one or two things they could pass on the way.

For older children
Encourage older children to examine published street maps and to add greater detail to their own map (bridges, crossroads, T-junctions).

Follow-up activities
▲ Look at local maps and try to find some of the children's homes.
▲ Make treasure maps to direct each other around the building to find a treasure of chocolate coins in a wooden box.
▲ Look at an Ordnance Survey map and follow the path of a river to the sea, tracing the route with a finger.

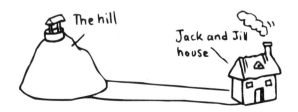

Bedtime

Objective
Art – to work practically and imaginatively with a variety of materials.

Group size
Small groups.

What you need
Card, scraps of material, wool, hole punch, a selection of sheets and blankets from a doll's pram or cot, a doll.

Preparation
Punch holes or cut lines in card to weave through. Cut up narrow strips of paper, card and material and cut lengths of wool and ribbon.

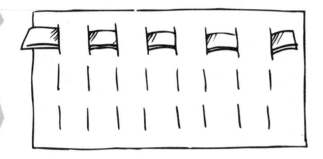

together the individual rectangles to make one large quilt for the doll.

Discussion
Talk about the different coverings the children have on their beds at home. Ask the children to tell you: How big are your covers? What colour are they? Compare them with the size of the coverings for the doll's cot. Which is the smallest? Why?

What to do
Encourage the children to think about what Jack needed to keep him warm when he was in bed. Supply the children with a variety of doll's blankets and sheets for them to examine what they are made out of and how they feel.

Explain to the children they are going to make a small cover for the doll (Jack). Introduce the materials to the children discussing which would be the most appropriate and colourful to use.

Provide some children with the holed card and explain they are to thread and tie different materials through the holes to create a colourful quilt for the doll.

Give the rest of the children a card for weaving and ask them to weave the various materials/card through the slits. Use the terms 'under and over' as they work.

Once all the weaving is complete join

For younger children
Supply the children with square pieces of card with holes around the edge. Encourage the children to thread laces or ribbons in and out of the holes.

For older children
Construct square looms using dowelling tied with wool. Provide the children with a selection of materials to tie onto the prepared loom.

Follow-up activities
▲ Make some simple looms out of plastic lids (such as from ice-cream containers) or paper plates.
▲ Weave through sacks used for onions or tangerines to create a colourful effect.
▲ Tie shades of blue/green material onto garden netting (available from garden centres or hardware stores) to represent sea or sky on a display board.

Tap, slap and flick

Objective
Music – to listen carefully and identify musical elements such as pitch and dynamics.

Group size
Small groups.

What you need
Chime bars, wood blocks, tambourine and baton.

Preparation
Group the children around you.

What to do
Choose one child to stand up and clap their hands, while the rest of the group listen. Ask the child to move to the other side of the room and clap again. Encourage the children to think about the differences they can hear, (the sound becomes quieter as you move away). Repeat the same process using different body parts such as snapping fingers, banging feet, slapping legs. Encourage the children to decide which sound is the loudest from a distance.

Ask the children: 'If Jack walked up the hill and Jill stayed at the bottom, would he be able to hear her talk?' If the children say he could not, ask them: 'How could she make herself heard?'

Explain to the children they are going to clap as they 'walk up the hill'. Discuss whether Jack would come down the hill at the same speed, faster or slower? Now clap Jack going up and coming down the hill faster. The children can repeat the same process either slapping their legs or snapping their fingers.

Introduce the children to the instruments, naming them and demonstrating the correct way to play them. Choose a child to play each instrument slowly to begin with and then getting faster. Use a baton to conduct whether they should play fast or slow.

Choose children to play the instruments and recite the nursery rhyme, slowly as they climb up the hill and quickly as they roll down the hill.

Discussion
Discuss with the children how the sound is carried through the air. If we face the wrong way, why can't we hear what is being said? What do we use to hear? Are all ears the same? Why do elephants have big ears?

For younger children
Encourage the children to sing the nursery rhyme tapping their hands and fingers both fast and slow, as Jack and Jill go up and down the hill. Ask the children to whisper or talk quietly to each other.

For older children
Listen to different types of music and discuss whether they are fast or slow. Lead the children in beating a rhythm which gets faster and faster, and then slows down.

Follow-up activities
▲ Listen to pieces of music which demonstrate sounds getting louder and quieter. Ask the children what the music makes them think of (trains coming into a station for example).
▲ Let the children take it in turns to be a conductor, using the baton to conduct the other children in. Try going faster and faster and then slower and slower.
▲ Test how far away a sound can be before the children stop hearing it. Try dropping a pin or whispering.

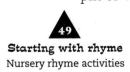

Hop, skip and a jump

Objective

PE – to travel using hands and feet, to link some actions and develop spatial awareness.

Group size

Large groups.

What you need

Tambourine and a large space to work.

Preparation

Reinforce the safety aspect of working in a confined space to the children, highlighting that they must avoid contact with others.

What to do

Warm-up

Encourage the children to move to the speed of the tambourine. Once the tambourine is struck the children fall down, repeat this several times.

Introduction

Explain to the children they must stride up the hill. When the tambourine is struck they are to fall down and roll like Jack tumbling down the hill. Repeat this, choosing different children to strike the tambourine.

Main activity

Ask the children to move about the room in different ways such as hopping, skipping, jumping, crawling. When the tambourine is struck they must fall and roll. Encourage the children to listen to the rhythm of the tambourine and move in time, from slow to fast to slow for example. Once again, when the tambourine is struck the children must fall down and roll (use recorded music if you prefer).

Explain to the

children they must put a sequence of movements together. For example a hop, fall, roll; skip, fall, roll; jump, fall, roll (changing the movement after each roll). Use demonstration to highlight good sequences.

Cool down

Play a simple game with the children, requiring them to move to command. For example, say: When I shout 'hill' you must walk; 'Jack' you must fall; 'Jill' you should roll and 'well' you must stretch.

Discussion

Discuss with the children which way they prefer to travel. How can they fall and jump quietly (landing on the balls of their feet and bending their knees). Talk about the different ways they can roll. Can you roll stretched out? Curled up? Backwards? Forwards? Which roll is the easiest?

For younger children

Provide plenty of opportunities for younger children to practice falling down as the tambourine is hit. Limit the sequencing aspect to two ways of travelling and rolling.

For older children

Encourage the children to work in pairs to shadow each other's movements. If available, the children could use apparatus to extend the activity.

Follow-up activities

▲ Draw pictures to hold up for the children to follow for the game in 'Cool down'.

▲ Challenge the children to devise a variety of action games, including rules to be played by the other children.

Circle of friends

Objective
RE – to learn to value friendships and to recognise each other's positive attributes.

Group size
Small groups.

What you need
Paper, scissors, drawing and colouring materials.

Preparation
Write out this poem on a large piece of paper in the shape of a person:

Make friends, make friends,
never, never, break friends.
Don't be nasty, just be kind,
be the best friend you can find.

What to do
Ask the children to stand in a circle holding hands and recite the poem. Discuss what friends are, what they do and why we need them. Encourage the children to use descriptive language such as caring, sharing, kind and helpful.

Ask the children to each name a friend and to say something positive about them (make sure everybody names and is named!). Give each child a piece of paper and ask them to draw their friend paying attention to the colour of eyes and hair.

Cut out the children's pictures and mount them with the hands stapled together to form a circle. Display these in a circle with the poem in the centre.

Discussion
Encourage the children to use appropriate language such as caring, sharing and kind.

Discuss other friendships in stories and nursery rhymes such as Piglet and Tigger and Hansel and Gretel.

For younger children
Instead of drawing pictures of their friends ask the children to make hand prints, in their friend's favourite colour and use these to form the circle.

For older children
The children can draw and write what they like to do together as friends. Attach the writing around the display or compile the work into a book.

Follow-up activities
▲ Tell stories about friends and dramatise them.
▲ Encourage the children to do a friendly task each day.
▲ Make a card to send to a friend or a passport-type card highlighting information about a friend.

Starting with rhyme
Nursery rhyme activities

Hospital beds

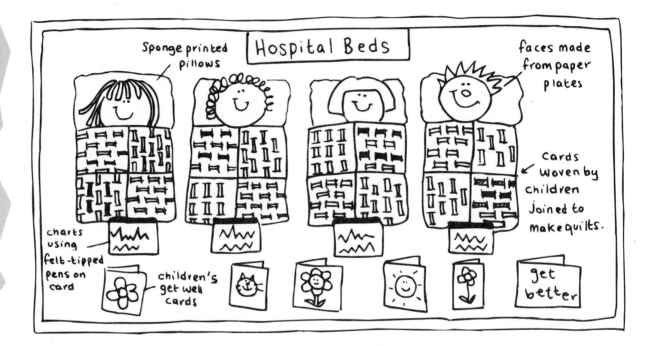

Sponge printed pillows

Hospital Beds

faces made from paper plates

cards woven by children joined to make quilts.

charts using felt-tipped pens on card

children's get well cards

get better

What you need

Paper plates, paper, card, pieces of material and paper cut into narrow strips to weave, sticky paper, wool, felt, glue, scissors, stapler and staples, paint, sponge, writing and colouring materials, card prepared for weaving (see page 48). Aprons and a covered work surface.

Preparation

Cover the work surface and make resources available to the children.

What to do

Organise groups of children to work on different sections of the display and then assemble the different parts.
Faces – ask four children to stick features on paper plates to create the heads for the patients. Use a variety of materials such as wool, sticky paper, felt and fabric.
Quilts – children can weave and tie materials onto prepared cards, as described on page 48. Join these together to make four quilts for the beds.
Pillows – ask four children to sponge-print

patterns onto rectangular pieces of paper.
Charts – organise four children to draw wavy lines with coloured felt-tipped pens onto squares of card.
Get well cards – make a variety of 'get well' cards either to the children's own design or prepared by you. Use these to create a border for the display.

Discussion

Remind the children about how Jack hurt himself and talk about the patients. Why do you think they are in bed? Could they get out of bed? What is wrong with them? When do you think they will go home? How do they eat their dinner? What are the charts at the bottom of the bed for?

Follow-up activities

▲ Make books for the 'patients' to read whilst they are in bed.
▲ Draw visitors to add to the display and change these daily. Label the visitors and the day they visit.
▲ Write an account of how the 'patients' came to be in hospital.

Up the hill

What you need
Paper, card, two pink circles, blue Cellophane, paint, scissors, glue, wool, felt, art straws, metallic paper (silver), wooden blocks in various sizes to print, string, three long cardboard tubes and collage materials, aprons and a covered work surface.

Preparation
Cover the work surface and make resources available. Cut out large letters for a heading – 'Jack and Jill went up the hill'.

What to do
Allocate different parts of the display to small groups of children.
Jack and Jill – create a head for Jack and a head for Jill, using pink circles and collage materials. Ask the children to draw outlines for the bodies and add collage materials.
Hill – ask two children to draw an outline of the hill, and stick art straws on for grass. This can then be sponged in shades of green.
Well – draw the base of the well and print to represent bricks. Now draw the roof of the well, print using smaller bricks. Paint the cardboard tubes, wrap string around them and assemble the well as shown below.

Buckets – ask the children to draw two buckets, one covered in blue Cellophane and the other half-covered. Make handles from metallic paper. Now draw and paint a fat and thin bucket, big and little, yellow and red bucket, outlined in metallic paper.
Print a blue background and attach the different sections as shown below. Label the various buckets appropriately.

Discussion
Ask the children: Which would be the easiest bucket to carry? Which would be the hardest to carry? What could you use instead of a bucket to carry the water?

Follow-up activities
▲ Challenge individual children to take measurements such as: hands, feet, arms, height and so on.
▲ Encourage the children to imagine specific details about Jack and Jill such as the colour of their eyes, hair and size. Make individual books about Jack and Jill.
▲ Investigate and record how many of Jill's small buckets it would take to fill Jack's big bucket. Record this information in a zigzag book as shown below.

Home-made lemonade

Group size
Small groups.

What you need
To make 900 ml/1½ pints you will need: two large lemons, 900 ml/1½ pints of boiling water, 400g sugar, one level teaspoon of citric acid. Aprons, hand washing facilities, covered work surface, measuring jug, kettle, lemon squeezer, scales and sieve.

Preparation
Ask the children to wash their hands using soap and to each put on an apron. Cover the work surface and place ingredients and equipment on the table.

What to do
Invite the children to help weigh and measure the ingredients. Boil the kettle, taking care to outline the hazards and dangers of boiling water and keeping the children well away from the kettle.

Peel, and squeeze the lemons and place the juice in a jug. Make sure an adult carefully adds the boiling water and sugar to the juice and lemon peel. This should be left overnight to infuse the flavour into the liquid. The next day use the sieve to strain, add citric acid and dilute with water.

Discussion
Discuss with the children when and why we drink lemonade. Encourage the children to realise that after exercise, such as a walk up a hill, they need a drink to prevent dehydration. Talk about the properties of the ingredients and any changes they go through. What does the lemon smell like? Why do we have to leave it overnight? Why does the lemonade need straining? What could you carry the lemonade in, if you wanted to take it with you on a walk? How many glasses of lemonade do you think Jack will drink?

Follow-up activities
▲ Invent some new drinks such as fruit juice cocktails or unusual milkshakes.
▲ Make swizzle sticks out of straws and cardboard to 'stir' the drinks.
▲ Plan some healthy food and drink for a group picnic.

▶ introduction ◀

Mary Mary Quite Contrary

Key G

Ma - ry, Ma - ry quite con - tra - ry, How does your gar - den grow? "With

sil - ver bells and co - ckle shells and pret - ty maids all in a row."

Most children enjoy playing out of doors, interacting with nature. Often this time is determined by the weather, and this rhyme provides an ideal opportunity to look at changes out of doors throughout the seasons. The activities throughout this section concentrate on growing and caring for gardens.

The children can observe the garden and how it changes over time, and can experiment with growing bulbs and seeds in varying conditions and naming the different parts of a plant.

Continue the garden theme as a basis for language activities, encouraging the children to develop and extend their vocabulary by describing in detail the flowers in Mary's garden.

Capture the children's imaginations by having a garden party to begin or conclude your activities. Use their organisational skills in deciding who is to be invited, how to do this, what is needed and when and where it will be held.

The host of colours and flowers that are found in the garden provides a firm basis for activities on colour recognition, matching activities and sequencing flowers and colours.

Once the children are familiar with the tune to 'Mary Mary', introduce percussion instruments to enhance the piece. Introduce these according to the ability and interest of the children, gradually working towards them performing independently as members of a group. Use chime bars and triangles throughout the rhyme to maintain the rhythm and when the children sing 'silver bells and cockle shells' shake the tambourine. Expand the structure further by encouraging the children to compose and perform a simple musical score linked to the weather.

Flower power

Objective
English – to develop speaking and listening skills and descriptive vocabulary .

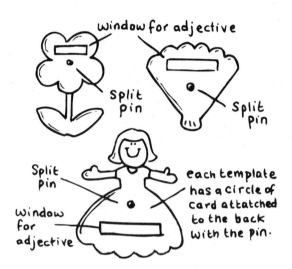

Group size
Small groups.

What you need
Selection of flowers and shells, card, paper, writing materials, split pins and a large copy of the nursery rhyme.

Preparation
Cut out large templates of a flower, shell and maid, complete with windows. Attach each one to a circular piece of card with split pins to form a rotating wheel.

What to do
Display the flowers and shells and ask the children what nursery rhyme it reminds them of. Using the large copy of the nursery rhyme, recite it together.

Focus on each of the three elements in turn: the flowers, shells and maids and ask the children to think of some words to describe them. Write the words down as they suggest them.

Introduce the wheeled flower first and explain that some describing words are needed to fill the window, so they can be seen as the wheel turns around. Help the children record some suitable words onto the wheels (pretty, colourful, spiky, beautiful, smelly).

Repeat the process for the shell and maid templates. Once completed these can be kept as a resource for the children to read.

Discussion
Take each object in turn, discussing some of their properties and features. What would the maids wear? What do they do in the garden? Where would you find flowers? What do you like about them? How do they smell? Where would you find shells? Who lives inside them? Do they feel the same both inside and out?

For younger children
Focus on flowers and make four different-shaped flower templates for recording the describing words, such as daffodils, roses, tulips, chrysanthemums.

For older children
Complete a similar activity but use flaps on the shells, flowers and maids to reveal the children's own descriptive words.

Follow-up activities
▲ Make some wheels to record other describing words.
▲ Describe other objects you may find in a garden, which the children could describe such as trees, ponds or toys.
▲ Talk about what would visit a bird table in your garden.

Come to a party

Objective
English – to write for a specific purpose.

Group size
Small groups.

What you need
Paper, drawing and writing materials, photocopiable sheet 93, scissors and a selection of printed invitations as examples.

Preparation
Photocopy page 93, enough for each child and cut and fold the invitations ready.

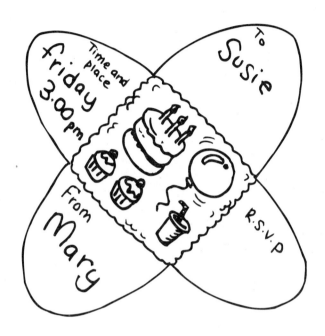

What to do
Explain to the children that Mary Mary is having a party in her garden and needs some help with the invitations. Discuss with the children an appropriate shape for the invitations.

Show the children the prepared invitation, encourage them to think about what is needed on the invite and why (time, place, date, to whom and from whom). Look at a selection of invitations for ideas.

Give each child the flower-shaped invitation to write on and ask them to fill it in carefully to invite a friend to Mary Mary's garden party.

When completed, place the invitation in an envelope and address it to a friend.

Discussion
Talk about the need to R.S.V.P. and what it means, show how one of the petals could be used for this purpose. Discuss with the children the purpose of addresses and what the different elements mean. What number house do you live in? What number is on the door of your friend's house? What's the name of your road? What town do you live in? Encourage the children to think about relating the invitation to the party (a petal because it's a garden party).

For younger children
Provide the children with a prepared invitation containing information about the party. The children have to address the invitation and sign their own name.

For older children
The children can design their own shaped invitation based upon some aspect of the nursery rhyme or garden party.

Follow-up activities
▲ Hold a party and write actual invitations.
▲ Send the children a teddy bear invitation for a teddy bears' picnic, asking them to R.S.V.P.
▲ Look closely at addresses, consider the value of postcodes and follow the journey of a letter.
▲ Encourage the children to write a menu for the teddy bears' picnic.

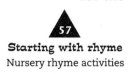

Next please

Objective
Mathematics – to use repeating patterns, recognise patterns and make predictions.

Group size
Large groups.

What you need
Card, coloured paint, sponges, drawing and colouring materials, clear adhesive film and paper.

Preparation
Make five red and five yellow flowers, five red and five yellow watering cans and five red and five yellow shells by drawing onto card, sponge painting, covering in clear adhesive film and cutting out.

What to do
Explain to the children that the 'pretty maids' in the nursery rhyme are going to be flowers in the garden. Choose six children to be 'flowers'. Ask them to stand in a row and ask alternate children to kneel, to create a pattern.

Give the six children a 'coloured flower', to make a pattern such as red, yellow, red, yellow and so on.

Repeat this exercise using the other visual aids to make different repeating patterns such as flower, watering can, flower, watering can; watering can, shell, watering can, shell and so on.

Invite the children to use the resource cards to make patterns and then to explain their patterns to the other children. Use the colour elements as well as the shapes.

Discussion
Talk about patterns in the environment. Do your curtains have patterns at home? Do any of your clothes have patterns on? Which is your favourite pattern? Can wallpapers have patterns? Can you make a pattern with beads, cotton reels or pegs?

For younger children
Ensure the children have plenty of practical experience copying and creating repeating

patterns, using everyday items such as pegs, beads and cotton reels.

For older children
Encourage older children to record the patterns made, and create more complex patterns, for example red, red, yellow, red, red, yellow and so on.

Follow-up activities
▲ Use a repeating pattern to make necklaces with beads.
▲ Create a repeating pattern for the children to follow around the room, such as red, blue, red, blue footprints.
▲ Print patterns to make a wallpaper border using a variety of printing tools such as blocks, circles and stickle bricks.

Mix and match

Objective
Mathematics – to match items one-to-one.

Group size
Small groups.

What you need
Card, drawing and writing materials, scissors and clear adhesive film.

Preparation
Make six different coloured maids, cutting a slit for the flowers to be held in their hands. Make eighteen flowers, three of each colour to match to the maid. Make six vases, coloured to match the maids and flowers. Cut out the maids, flowers and vases and cover them all with clear adhesive film.

What to do
Ask the children to match a coloured flower to the same coloured vase. Repeat this process until all the flowers are in vases. Introduce the 'pretty maids', telling the children to transfer the flowers from the vases to the same coloured maid. Now jumble the flowers into the wrong coloured maid and ask the children if they can rearrange them.

Next take away some of the maids and group the flowers in a vase, asking the children: Are there more maids than flowers? Ask the children to estimate which is the greater number and check by matching the maids to the flowers.

Repeat this activity using different numbers of maids, flowers and vases.

Discussion
Discuss with the children other examples of matching: knife, fork and spoon for each person at the table; socks and shoes. Pose questions such as: What could you match with a bucket? What could you match with an umbrella?

cut slit for flower

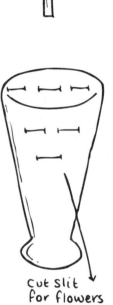
cut slit for flowers

For younger children
Within a role-play setting provide 'real experiences' for the children to match, asking a child to give the doll a teddy bear.

For older children
Provide opportunities for the children to match more obscure objects. Use matching activities as a basis for addition

Follow-up activities
▲ Use the visual aids to develop addition skills: 'If we have three green flowers how many red flowers do we need to make five flowers altogether?'
▲ Introduce number bonds, using the visual aids to discover different ways to make five.

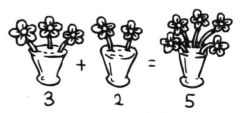

3 + 2 = 5

▲ **59**
Starting with rhyme
Nursery rhyme activities

Grow and show

Objective
Science – to name external parts of plants and identify properties of living things.

Group size
Small groups.

What you need
Selection of bulbs (daffodil, snowdrop, hyacinth, tulip, bluebell, crocus), magnifying glasses, pots, compost, water, bulb grower, lollipop sticks, pictures or drawings of flowering bulbs, newspaper and spoons, washing-up bowl.

Preparation
Mount the pictures onto card, cover a table with newspaper and place compost in the washing-up bowl. Sit the children in a circle, displaying the bulbs in the centre.

What to do
Before you begin, make sure the children are clear that they must not put the bulbs near their mouths. Wash hands after handling bulbs. Ask a child to choose a bulb and to pass it around the circle. Encourage the children to describe the bulb (hard, little, smooth, pointed). Repeat this, considering all the bulbs and their properties in turn. Ask the children what will happen if you plant it? What will it grow into?

Ask the children to sort the bulbs into sets (little, big, dark brown, round). Discuss with the children what they think the flower will look like, asking them to match the bulbs to the pictures. Encourage the children to think about whether the size of the bulb is related to the size of the flower.

Ask the children what bulbs need to grow? Following the children's instructions, plant the bulbs spooning the compost into the pot, and watering it. Use lollipop sticks to label the pots.

Place the bulb in a bulb grower to watch the roots and shoots grow, use appropriate language to describe what you can see whenever possible. Using a drawing of the parts of a flower, discuss the names and parts of the plant (roots, stem, shoot, bud, leaf, stalk).

Discussion
Discuss with the children why plants need certain things to grow. Why do they need water and food? What happens if they do not get water and food? Are they living things? Do all flowers grow from bulbs? What else could we try and grow?

For younger children
Limit the types of bulbs to two. Plant quick-growing seeds such as cress or beansprouts to provide more instant results.

For older children
Invite older children to investigate the growth of beans in jars using damp kitchen roll. Measure and record their growth.

Follow-up activities
▲ Lay a potato in a shoe box maze with a window at the opposite end to see how the roots grow.
▲ Experiment with growth conditions by placing cress in different settings (such as, in the dark, no water, in the cold, or with no cotton wool).
▲ Plant hamster food or wild bird seed to see what happens.
▲ Make grass heads by cutting the feet out of tights, filling them with compost and grass seeds, securing the ends with elastic bands and watering regularly. Ask the children to attach features using their choice of different materials.

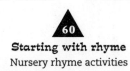

Grow plant, grow

Objective
Design and Technology – to make a pop-up toy.

Group size
Small groups.

What you need
Card, plastic cups, dowelling, drawing and colouring materials, glue, scissors and Sellotape.

Preparation
Cover a work surface and cut dowelling into small pieces (approximately 20cm). Place a small hole in the bottom of each cup. Plant in pots a selection of seeds or bulbs, to demonstrate the growth of plants.

What to do
Talk to the children about how the plants in Mary's garden grew, and how they grow in a plant pot. Look closely at previously planted seeds and bulbs.

Show the children the selection of resources available, explaining they are going to make a 'pop-up' plant and ask for suggestions as to how it can be done.

Following this, demonstrate to the children how to make the plant 'pop up'. Ask the children to draw and cut out a simple flower shape on card which they can colour in. Attach these to the end of a piece of dowelling and insert the dowelling through the paper cup. Wrap some Sellotape around the stick to protect the children's fingers. Let the children complete as much of the task as possible, offering adult help only when necessary.

Let the children practise popping their flowers up and down!

Discussion
Discuss with the children: What makes the plant 'pop up' or 'down'? Discuss why the dowelling used has to be circular rather than square. Ask the children to think about what else a lever could be used for.

For younger children
Provide the children with a template of a flower to cut out and attach to the dowelling.

For older children
Develop the activities further and encourage the children to try using levers made from card.

Follow-up activities
▲ Make different 'pop-up' people and animals and hold conversations!
▲ Use construction kits to make things move up and down.

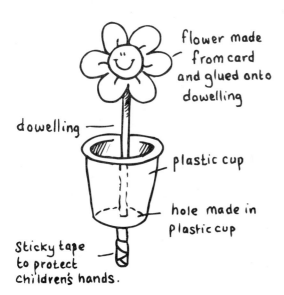

flower made from card and glued onto dowelling

dowelling

plastic cup

hole made in plastic cup

Sticky tape to protect children's hands.

Changing time

Objective
History – to sequence events to develop a sense of chronology.

Group size
Small groups.

What you need
Pictures of garden activities (swings, slides, football, skipping, making snowmen, flying a kite, playing in the paddling pool), paper, drawing and colouring materials.

Preparation
Ensure the children know the names of the different seasons and the different types of weather that occur at these times, as well as the sequence in which the seasons occur. Discuss with the children the changes that they think would occur in Mary's garden through the seasons.

What to do
Show the children each picture in turn, discussing what's happening. Ask the children to name when the different activities would take place by associating them to the different weather of the seasons.

Challenge the children to place the pictures in sequence starting with winter time (building snowmen in winter, skipping in spring, playing in the paddling pool in summer and flying a kite in autumn).

Discussion
Ask questions such as: In which season will Mary's garden be full of flowers? In which season will Mary's garden have no flowers growing? In which season would the bulbs need to be planted in Mary's garden? What do flowers grow from?

For younger children
Focus on winter and summer, stressing the differences – what the weather is like, what activities children might do, where they go, what they wear and so on.

For older children
Keep a diary to record the changes in activities throughout the seasons.

Follow-up activities
▲ Take photographs of a garden throughout the four seasons; arrange these into a timeline.
▲ Consider the 'flowering garden' throughout the four seasons; when they need sowing, when they flourish, when they wither and die.
▲ Study gardens in the past and find out how land was used (kitchen gardens, lawns for croquet, herb gardens).

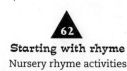

What's the weather like today?

Objective
Geography – to observe, recognise and record changes in the weather.

sunny

cloudy

lightning

raining

windy

snowing

Group size
Small groups.

What you need
Selection of clothes for various weather conditions (umbrella, woolly hat, shorts, T-shirt, sun hat, woolly scarf, gloves, wellingtons, anorak), paper, drawing and colouring materials, card and weather maps cut from newspapers.

Preparation
Draw examples of weather symbols onto card, mount weather maps. Arrange the children in a circle around the selection of clothes.

What to do
Ask a child to choose an item of clothing, to name what it is and say when they think they would wear it and why. Repeat the same process with each item of clothing in turn.

Let the children make sets of clothes worn in different weather types, such as T-shirt, shorts and sun hat for a sunny day. Discuss with the children what they would wear today and why, focusing upon what the weather is like.

Encourage the children to think of ways/symbols to represent the different types of weather. Following this, introduce the prepared symbols asking them who may use them and where else they may have seen them. Show the children the weather maps, complete with symbols.

Explain to the children that they are to record the weather each day to create a weather chart by drawing a picture of the weather with a symbol underneath. Date these and display them to form a picture of the weather over a set period of time.

Discussion
Ask the children: What kind of weather would help the flowers in Mary's garden grow? Do flowers grow in all types of weather? When wouldn't the flowers grow in Mary's garden? What would happen if you were dressed for a sunny day in the winter? What would happen if you were dressed for a winter's day in the summer? Which is your favourite type of weather? Why do you like it best? What do you do in different kinds of weather?

For younger children
Following the initial discussion, make a weather wheel and ask the children to change it daily.

For older children
Introduce temperature and show the children how to record this using a thermometer. Make individual weather charts over a set period of time. Make a rainfall gauge to record the amount of rain.

Follow-up activities
▲ Make windsocks and windmills to demonstrate wind direction.
▲ Look at barometers and other weather gauges.
▲ Link the weather types to the seasons and point out the cycle this follows.
▲ Look at weather patterns in different countries,

▲ 63
Starting with rhyme
Nursery rhyme activities

Dib, dab, flowers

Objective
Art – to appreciate the work of other artists and experiment with visual elements.

Explain to the children they are going to be artists and create their own pictures using methods like Van Gogh and Monet.

Consider the vase of flowers, placed in the centre of the table. Encourage the children to paint a picture using dabs and swirls of different coloured finger paint to represent the petals, stalk, leaves and background. Stress to the children that all the background should be filled in as well.

Discussion
Talk to the children about the type and colour of flowers you would find in Mary's garden. What new colours can we make from the coloured finger paints? What would you like to have in the background of your picture? Do you think Monet and Van Gogh used their fingers? What are you going to call your picture?

For younger children
Ask the children to concentrate on painting just the flower heads using their fingers to dab on their paint.

For older children
Provide the children with different tools to attempt to apply the paint using similar techniques to Monet and Van Gogh.

Follow-up activities
▲ Look at the work of a variety of artists and consider the techniques and subject matter chosen.
▲ Use different tools to print to create other shaped petals such as dahlias.
▲ Display the children's pictures together to make a large garden picture; superimpose 'Mary Mary' on the top.

Group size
Small groups.

What you need
Finger paints (red, blue, yellow, black and white), paper, water, soap, paper towels, examples of work by Monet and Van Gogh showing flowers and a selection of real flowers in a vase.

Preparation
Mount and display pictures, cover work surface and arrange paints.

What to do
Display the prints of paintings and look closely with the children at them, highlighting things such as the colours and the techniques used (dotting, swirling, shape) and size.

Crash, bang, shine

Objective
Music – to begin to record and compose simple music pieces.

Group size
Small groups.

What you need
Selection of musical instruments (tambourines, triangles, cymbals, bells, wood blocks, drums, maracas, wooden and metal guiros), photocopiable page 94, drawing materials and card.

Preparation
Ask the children to sit in a circle around the instruments. Copy enough sheets for each child to have one and mount a large copy of it onto card.

What to do
Choose a child to pick an instrument and ask them to play it, describe the sound it makes and say what it reminds them of to the other children. Repeat this process with each instrument in turn.

Recite the nursery rhyme together, asking the children to think about the different sounds made and if any of these can be related to weather sounds heard in the garden (tapping the tambourine sounds like the rain). Provide opportunities for the children to experiment with a variety of instruments.

Give the children an instrument each, grouping them by weather sounds. Display the large score and choose a child to point to a weather symbol. As the child points to the weather symbol, those children with the appropriate instruments play them. Repeat this several times to develop the

children's confidence.
Give each child a photocopied sheet and ask them to select and draw an appropriate instrument for each weather symbol. Now in pairs the children can repeat the activity, using their own musical score.

Discussion
Talk about dynamics and tempo: Is the rain always loud? When is it quiet? Does it come down fast or slow? Would you play the sun music fast or slow? When would it need to be fast?

For younger children
Limit the choice of instruments and guide them to those which make very obvious weather-like sounds. Use an enlarged version of the score or adapt it to contain only two different types of weather.

For older children
Encourage the children to create their own score, develop the pace elements so that the conductor achieves a detailed musical effect.

Follow-up activities
▲ Create other musical scores using different stimuli such as animal noises.
▲ Perform the nursery rhyme to music.
▲ Tell a story about different weather days, compose a piece of music to accompany it and record it onto tape.

Picking flowers

Objective
PE – to develop spatial awareness, colour recognition, sending and travelling skills.

Group size
Large group.

What you need
Selection of coloured hoops to represent vases (approximately six of each colour), coloured bean bags to represent flowers (at least two per child) and a tambourine.

Preparation
Along the four sides of the room place the hoops in a coloured sequence, for example: red, blue, yellow, green. Scatter the bean bags in the middle of the floor.

What to do
Encourage the children to walk about the space avoiding squashing the 'flowers'. When you hit the tambourine each child has to walk to a 'flower', pick it up, then walk to the same coloured 'vase' and put the flower in the 'vase'.

Repeat this activity several times changing the way the children travel, for example: skip around the flowers, hop, jump and then gallop. Once the children have grown in confidence with this game, develop it further, allowing the children to practise their sending skills by standing still when the tambourine is hit and carefully tossing the 'flowers' to the appropriate 'vase'.

Discussion
Give the children opportunities to discuss different directions and ways of travelling using different parts of their body including forwards, backwards, sideways, running, crawling, two feet and one hand, two hands and one foot.

For younger children
Ask the children to collect the 'flowers' and put them in any coloured 'vase'.

For older children
Ask the children to travel to the 'vase' placing the 'flower' on a different part of their body each time (shoulder, head).

Follow-up activities
▲ Link together two different ways of travelling around the 'flowers'.
▲ Adapt the game by adding different dimensions: Here comes the rain, crouch down low. Here comes the sun, spread out your arms.
▲ Develop sending and receiving skills using hoops and bean bags.

▲ 66 ▲
Starting with rhyme
Nursery rhyme activities

Take care

Objective
RE – to develop a sense of responsibility for living things.

Group size
Small groups.

What you need
Selection of cut flowers, vase, food colouring and flowering plants.

Preparation
Colour the water by adding a few drops of food colouring (check for permanency).

What to do
Talk with the children about how Mary would look after her garden and what she would need to give the flowers to help them grow. Discuss the idea that sometimes flowers look nice in the house, but that these cut flowers still need to be taken care of. Ask the children how this is done.

Demonstrate to the children how flowers take water, by placing the cut flowers in a vase of coloured water and observing what happens.

Can the children think of other ways in which we look after flowers and plants both indoors and out?

Discussion
Ask the children which is their favourite colour to change the flowers into. Ask the children what is the difference between weeds and plants in the garden? What do weeds do? Talk about other things we take responsibility for and look after, such as animals and pets.

For younger children
Provide opportunities for the children to look after a plant or flowers in your room or plant bulbs outside in a 'garden area' for the children to look after.

For older children
Provide each child with a partner, other than their friend to care for and play with during the day.

Follow-up activities
▲ Provide cut-out card 'petals' for the children to add to a card 'flower head' each time they show a friend they care.
▲ Make lists to describe how to care for a friend, a pet or living thing.
▲ Look at the way flowers are used to say 'thank you', 'I love you' or 'sorry'.

Garden centre

What you need
Paper, card, glue, Sellotape, tissue paper, colouring and writing materials, sawdust/sand, plastic bags, stapler, rice, old tights, containers, paint, selection of shapes.

Preparation
Cover work surface and place resources in an accessible position for the children.

What to do
Discuss the kinds of things that might be found at a garden centre. If possible take the children to visit one. If this is not possible provide a selection of objects for them to see. Allocate the following tasks to groups of children:

Seed packets: use pieces of paper pre-folded to form a packet. Draw pictures of flowers on the front. Write planting instructions on the back and glue the sides. Put a few grains of rice inside as seeds and stick down.

Bulbs: cut the feet off old pairs of tights and stuff the toes with paper to represent the bulbs. Place these in a container. Write 'bulbs' on the side and decorate with flowers.

Compost: fill plastic bags with sawdust or sand to represent compost. Make labels, showing its name and what it is used for, before placing it in a container, to sell.

Plant pots: cover used containers with paper and decorate them.

Flower books: staple several sheets of paper together to make a book. Draw a different flower on each page, add some writing.

Flowers: stick coloured circles of tissue paper onto straws. Display in a tray of sand.

Wrapping paper: print sheets of wrapping paper using paint and a variety of shapes.

Plants: push twigs into self drying clay, then decorate with green tissue for leaves.

Signs: make labels for the wall, showing price lists and examples of things on sale.

Discussion
Talk to the children about things sold in garden centres. What do they think would be the most popular things and why? What is the difference between flowers and vegetables? What is the difference between seeds and bulbs?

Follow-up activities
▲ Create a café and gift shop to go alongside the garden centre.
▲ Make activity cards to use in the garden centre saying, for example buy two plants, a bunch of flowers and some daffodil bulbs.
▲ Plant a garden outside or sow plants to sell in the garden centre.

Whatever the weather

What you need
Paper, card, sponges, split pins, wire wool, paints, writing and colouring materials, shapes to print, glue, gold glitter, cotton wool, tissue paper and shiny gold paper.

Preparation
Cover the work surface and separate the display board into two parts.

What to do
Allocate the children different tasks:
Spring – print chicks using yellow paint and different sized circles, painting the beak in orange and the legs and an eye in black. Draw the outline of lambs and stick cotton wool on for fleece. Mount the chicks and lambs onto green paper circles. Make daffodils for a border by printing petals using a pre-cut sponge and attaching a piece of yellow tissue rolled into a tube.
Summer – draw an outline of a large sun. Stick shiny gold paper onto it and sprinkle with gold glitter. Mix yellow paint with glue and use circles, rectangles or triangles to print small suns for a border.
Autumn – paint a tree trunk using brown paint with glue. Drag wire wool through the wet paint to give a rough bark effect. Sponge print leaves on the branches using red, orange, yellow and brown paint. Make mounds of leaves for the base of the tree using scrunched up tissue paper and print leaves onto it. Print leaves in a variety of colours for the border.
Winter – draw Jack Frost, using black and blue paint, to give a spiky effect. Cut out silver triangles and stick them to his arms and legs to represent icicles. Use paint and circles to print snowmen for a border.

Cut out the seasons' names in suitable colours, such as 'Winter' in silver paper.

Assemble the display as shown below. Attach an arrow to show the present season.

Choose a child each day to draw a picture to represent the weather. Mount and display the pictures with the day and date.

Discussion
Ask the children: Which is your favourite season? What do you wear when it is hot? How many sunny days have there been?

Follow-up activities
▲ Make up a story for each of the seasons.
▲ Record the weather over several months

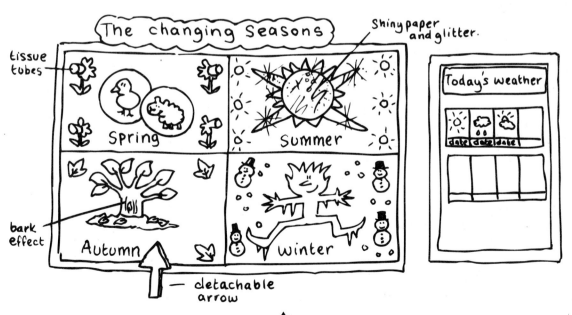

tissue tubes

bark effect

The changing Seasons

Shiny paper and glitter.

Spring   Summer

Autumn   Winter

Today's weather

date date date

— detachable arrow

Flower cake

Group size
Small groups.

What you need
Large cake tin, 250g margarine, 250g caster sugar, 250g self raising flour, 4 eggs, mixer, bowl, knife, oven, greaseproof paper, cake board, green colouring, desiccated coconut.

To decorate: 200g margarine and 375g sieved icing sugar for butter cream, 'Liquorice Allsorts', candy sticks, chocolate buttons, jelly diamonds, sugar flowers or stars, chocolate fairy drops, chocolate fingers, 'Hundreds and Thousands', silver balls.

Preparation
Set oven to 180°C. Grease and line tin. Cream margarine and sugar to make butter cream. Turn the coconut green by placing in a bag with green food colouring and shaking. Cover work surface, place sweets in dishes.

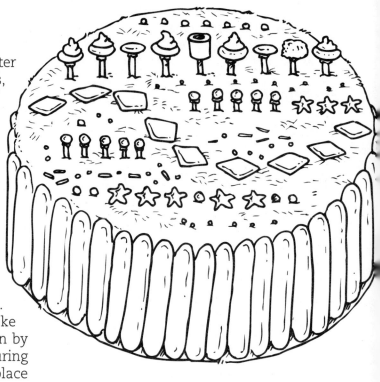

What to do
Make sponge cake by creaming margarine and caster sugar together, adding eggs and mixing, sieve in flour and stir. Place in prepared baking tin and cook for 30 minutes or until golden brown and springy.

Once cool, place on cake board and cover the surface of the cake in butter cream. Stick chocolate fingers around the edge of the cake and sprinkle green coconut on the top of the cake.

Make a curved pathway across the cake using the jelly diamonds. To make rows of flowers attach chocolate buttons or fairy drops with butter cream to liquorice or candy sticks, and place in rows on cake.

Attach silver balls on candy sticks with butter cream and place in rows on the cake to make silver bells. Arrange sugar flowers or stars in rows to represent the cockle shells in the garden. Share the cake out.

Discussion
Ask the children: What else would you have in your garden? What do gardeners use? Where could their tools be kept and why? Would you have a table and chairs in your garden? Would you need an umbrella, if so why? Could you make a patio on your 'garden'? What type of sweets would you use? Where would you position them?

Follow-up activities
▲ Make fairy cakes and decorate each with different 'flowers'.
▲ Make a Hansel and Gretel secret cottage using the same type of cake and sweets to decorate.
▲ Try making a vegetable garden using moulded icing or marzipan to make the different vegetables.

chapter five
▶ introduction ◀

Humpty Dumpty

Key C

Hump - ty Dump - ty sat on a wall. Hump - ty Dump - ty had a great fall.

All the King's hors - es and all the King's men, Could - n't put Hump - ty to - geth - er a - gain.

Humpty Dumpty is a popular nursery rhyme with children of all ages. The activities in this chapter focus on the traditional version but there are many variations involving Humpty Dumpty in different settings, with many different characters, and completing different activities, with which children will often be familiar. This highlights the range of opportunities for children to devise their own rhymes based on Humpty Dumpty.

Some children may be unaware that Humpty Dumpty is actually an egg! Encourage all the children to find out about which animals produce eggs, how they are hatched, their size, shape and further properties.

Explain to the children how versatile eggs are and provide opportunities for them to experience cooking and tasting eggs which have been boiled, fried, scrambled, poached or mixed with other ingredients to make cakes, pancakes, and so on.

Humpty Dumpty is valuable for developing children's empathy. It provides opportunities to consider Humpty's feelings and emotions in relation to their own. The rhyme helps to foster a caring, sharing and loving attitude towards others.

The tune consists of repeating patterns which develop a strong sense of structure, enabling the children to keep pace and the rhyme also lends itself to the use of percussion instruments at key points. Use cymbals to create a crescendo, representing Humpty Dumpty's actual fall from the wall, the wood blocks to create the sounds of the horses hooves, and the xylophone to accompany the piano or guitar.

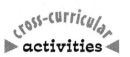

All together now 1, 2, 3

Objective
English – to participate as a speaker and listener in a group situation.

Group size
Small groups.

What you need
Tape recorder, short blank tapes, card, paper, drawing and colouring materials, plastic wallets, large and small copies of a variety of nursery rhymes and songs ('Humpty Dumpty', 'Jack and Jill', 'Mary Mary quite contrary', 'Hickory dickory dock').

Preparation
Prepare a small copy of each of the nursery rhymes onto card for the children to use

individually and one large copy of 'Humpty Dumpty'.

What to do
Using the large copy of 'Humpty Dumpty' recite the nursery rhyme together, pointing to the words as the children sing. Provide an individual copy of the nursery rhyme for each child in the group and ask them to carefully illustrate it. Ask two children to illustrate the large copy of Humpty Dumpty.

Using the individual copies of the rhyme, ask the children to 're-read' the nursery rhyme together. Repeat this process at least twice recording the children's voices onto the short blank tapes.

Place the tapes and nursery rhyme cards in plastic wallets in the listening area,

labelling the tape, wallet and nursery rhyme to be used by the children at future dates.

Discussion
Talk about the nature of the illustrations. Why draw them on the cards? What service do they provide? What would be appropriate to draw? Talk to the children about the importance of them representing the rhyme, so it can be 'read' from the pictures.

For younger children
Recite Humpty Dumpty with the children, and provide pre-illustrated cards for the children to colour.

For older children
Invite the children to record the nursery rhyme individually, encouraging them to change the expression and tone of their voices. Ask the children to introduce themselves and the nursery rhyme before reciting the rhyme, giving their age, name, what they like and don't like, say what the rhyme is about and so on.

Follow-up activities
▲ Make visual aids to support the nursery rhyme; a wall, Humpty Dumpty and the king's men to attach to the wall with Velcro.
▲ Record stories onto blank tapes for the children to follow in the books.
▲ Devise your own stories, illustrate them and record them onto tapes to listen to.

Draw a wall

Objective
English – to develop phonetic language, word association and spelling.

Group size
Small groups.

What you need
Large picture of a wall, examples of rhyming pictures (cat/mat, sun/bun, bin/tin), copy of 'Humpty Dumpty' nursery rhyme, scissors, card, writing materials.

Preparation
Display the 'wall' and a copy of the nursery rhyme for the children to see.

What to do
Recite the nursery rhyme together, looking closely at and pointing to the rhyming words as you sing.

Alter the nursery rhyme by changing some of the text and encouraging the children to insert a rhyming word. For example sing 'Humpty Dumpty sat on a pig' or 'Humpty Dumpty did a jig'.

Provide plenty of opportunities for the children to hear these rhyming words, as well as making their own, in order to change the nursery rhyme.

Choose each child in turn to draw pairs of rhyming pictures. Scribe the words, highlighting the word structure.

Attach these to the wall to form rhyming bricks. Once the children become familiar with this, challenge them further into thinking of more rhyming family words starting with hat, cat, sat, mat for example. Record these either in pictures or in written form to add to the rhyming wall.

Discussion
As this is mainly a discussion-based activity ensure all the children take a turn and respect each other's ideas. Talk about poetry with the children and mention how the poet often makes the words rhyme. Ask the children to think of the benefits of rhyme. Does it add to the enjoyment of a poem?

For younger children
Provide the children with sets of pictures from which there are rhyming words. Encourage the children to play snap type games with these.

For older children
Provide opportunities for the children to think of rhyming sentences such as a pig with a wig or the cat sat on the mat. Children could then work in pairs, making sentences for each other, but omitting the rhyming word and asking their partner to insert a suitable word.

Follow-up activities
▲ Make more complicated rhyming words using vowel changes, such as coat/goat.
▲ Shape the bricks of the wall into jigsaw pieces for the children to use as a resource.

What size?

Objective
Mathematics – to develop mathematical vocabulary and to make comparisons.

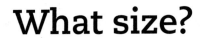

Group size
Small groups.

What you need
Large wooden or plastic blocks and Unifix cubes, construction kits such as Duplo, LEGO, Sticklebricks. Sponge ball, paper, glue, drawing and colouring materials, plant pot or margarine tub.

Preparation
Ensure that the children have had plenty of practise using the construction materials which are available. They should also be familiar with the nursery rhyme. Make Humpty Dumpty by attaching concertina arms and legs with glue to the sponge ball. Colour, cut and stick on features and sit him on a plant pot or margarine tub to stop him rolling away.

What to do
Discuss with the children what type of wall Humpty Dumpty sat on in the rhyme. Introduce and develop language such as tall, short, high, low.

Show the children your own Humpty Dumpty and together with the children make a wall tall enough for him to sit on. Challenge the children to work in pairs to make a taller and then a shorter wall for Humpty Dumpty. Once they have tried this discuss with the children which is the tall, taller and tallest wall and make labels for each wall. Repeat the same process for short, shorter and shortest.

Explain to the children that the wall must now fit 'all the king's men' on – so it must be longer. Encourage them to make a long wall using a different construction kit.

Discussion
Talk to the children about the structure of walls. How do walls interlink? What are walls made from? Why don't walls fall down? How can you make walls stronger? How safe are walls?

For younger children
Provide opportunities for the children to have plenty of free play with the construction kits. Encourage them to think about tall and short walls, and to look for things in the environment which are taller or shorter than themselves.

For older children
Encourage the children to determine a way of measuring the height and length of the walls using a non-standard measurement (such as their hands or feet).

Follow-up activities
▲ Extend the activity into other play areas, making long, short and tall walls in the sand tray or with play dough.
▲ Introduce standard units of measure to determine the height and length of the wall.
▲ Make bricks from self-drying clay and challenge the children to build their own walls. Investigate ways of 'cementing' the bricks together.

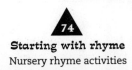

Horses and jockeys

Objective
Mathematics – to develop ordering skills and colour knowledge through a game.

Group size
Groups of six.

What you need
Large and small card, coloured dice, drawing and colouring materials, clear adhesive film, photocopiable page 95.

Preparation
Make a base board by enlarging photocopiable page 95 to A3 and pasting onto a large sheet of card; colour in each column a different colour to match the colours on the dice. Cut out six coloured horse's heads on card (matching the colours to the colours on the dice), using the picture on the board as a guide. Make a Humpty Dumpty sitting on a wall out of card to be placed at the end of the base board. Cover the board with clear adhesive film.

What to do
Explain to the children that Humpty is about to fall off his wall and someone needs to help him. Ask the children which coloured horse they think will reach Humpty first.

The children must take it in turns to throw the dice and move the corresponding horse one horseshoe forward. Carry on until one horse wins by reaching Humpty.

Discussion
As the game is being played ask the children: Which horse is coming first, second or third? What is a jockey? What does a jockey do? What do horses eat? How fast do horses travel? How tall are horses? How are horses measured?

For younger children
With a group of younger children you will need to take a more active role in the game and could join in yourself. Limit the number of horses and players to three by altering the dice to show two faces with each colour.

For older children
Encourage the children to keep a record of the horses' movements. The children could determine how many horseshoes ahead the winning horse was.

Follow-up activities
▲ Alter the rules to create a new game; using a numbered and coloured dice to determine how many horseshoes forwards to move the coloured horse.
▲ Make a new board game based upon Humpty Dumpty or another nursery rhyme.
▲ Write a story to describe the race; what happened to the horses and jockeys and what happened at the end of the race.

▲ 75
Starting with rhyme
Nursery rhyme activities

Eggs-change

Objective

Science – to find out and predict what happens to eggs when they are heated.

Group size
Small groups.

What you need
Eggs, pan, frying pan, knife, wooden spoon, dish, cooker, paper plates, paper, card, split pins, drawing and colouring materials.

Preparation
Cut two pieces of card into egg shapes, make zigzag cuts across one of the 'eggs' and attach to the other egg with split pins. Arrange the group of children in a circle.

What to do
Carefully pass an egg around the circle, encouraging each child to say one thing about it. Link the idea of the egg to Humpty Dumpty and ask the children if the same thing might happen to the egg as happened to Humpty Dumpty? Break the egg into a dish, and repeat the above process of describing the egg.

Introduce the egg-shaped recording sheet. Record the words which the children used to describe the whole egg on the outside, and the words to describe the broken egg on the inside.

Ask the children if the egg could be changed, and if so how?

Show the children how an egg can be cooked, stressing that the heat changes the egg. Make sure the children are seated away from your cooking source at a safe distance.

Start by frying an egg until it is cooked and placing the cooked egg on a paper plate next to the uncooked egg. Invite the children to look at the two eggs and compare the differences in texture and appearance.

Question the children as to what will happen if we crack the egg into hot water. Poach the egg in this way for the children to test their predictions.

Ensure an egg is fried, boiled, scrambled and poached for the children to make comparisons between texture, appearance and taste. Make labels and display with the cooked eggs.

Discussion
Talk to the children about the properties of eggs. Do they roll? Can you roll them in a straight line? Do they float? Are they strong or fragile?

For younger children
Focus on one type of eggs (boiled eggs) asking the children to predict the differences in an egg boiled for a short and a long time.

For older children
Provide an egg-shaped book, similar to the record sheet for each child to record the process used to change the eggs.

Follow-up activities
▲ Make a graph to show the favourite way to eat eggs.

▲ Try another food and find out what happens when it is heated; look at hard blocks of chocolate, find out what happens when it is heated, and then cooled again.

▲ Consider different sized and types of eggs: ostrich, duck, hen, goose, quail, looking particularly at external features.

Sat on a wall

Objective
Design and Technology – to use a range of materials to make a jointed model.

Group size
Small groups.

What you need
Paper, card, split pins, Sellotape, glue, Blu-Tack, string, paper-clips, stapler and staples, paint, blocks or sponges to print with, variety of collage materials, collection of eggs (Easter, chocolate, hens, foil), writing and drawing materials.

Preparation
Cover the work surface and place the materials in an accessible position.

Explain to the children they are going to make a Humpty Dumpty sitting on a wall. Consider with the children the different colours and types of eggs, enabling them to decide the most suitable materials for their own Humpty Dumpty. Look at some walls around your setting or in pictures to identify the patterns they make, the way the bricks interlock and the colours used.

What to do
Provide each child with a piece of card and ask them to print a wall using wooden blocks or sponges, remembering the patterns which they have seen. Provide a second piece of card and encourage the children to draw a Humpty Dumpty shape, taking note of the size of their wall.

Once they have drawn the basic shape let the children use the available collage materials to decorate their work. Ensure that the children remember to add facial features, arms and legs.

Once Humpty Dumpty and the wall are complete, talk about the different ways of attaching him to the wall. Make available a variety of fasteners and allow the children to fasten Humpty Dumpty to the wall, securely in an appropriate position.

Talk to the children about the best fastener to give Humpty Dumpty the most mobility (split pins).

Discussion
Talk to the children about the rhyme and their models. Why do we need to make Humpty Dumpty move? In which part of the nursery rhyme would Humpty Dumpty be up, and which part would he be down?

For younger children
Provide the children with a template of Humpty Dumpty. Ask them to add collage materials. Demonstrate the different ways the fasteners can be used before asking the children to choose an appropriate method.

For older children
Present the children with opportunities to attach other things to the wall such as the king's horses and the king's men.

Follow-up activities
▲ Make an egg with a fold down flap to reveal a broken egg inside.
▲ Make horses with moving legs.
▲ Design and make puppets to re-enact the nursery rhyme.

Cars or horses

Objective

History – to look at change over time, to use artefacts to learn about the past.

Group size
Small groups.

What you need
Large cloth bag, two smaller identical cloth bags, toy car, toy or picture of a petrol pump, car tyre from a construction kit, car keys, toy horse, small bag of hay, horseshoe or picture of horseshoe, black paper and white labels.

Preparation
Make a magic wand by rolling the black paper into a narrow tube shape and securing it with sticky labels, one on each end. Place 'car' articles in one small bag and 'horse' articles in the other, place the 'horse' bag inside the large bag.

What to do
Show the children the bag containing the 'car' articles. Let them look inside to determine what the items are and ask them how they would be used. Once the concept of the car as a means to travel has been grasped, place this bag inside the large bag. Choose a child to wave the 'wand' and ask them all to say: 'wave your wand, now wave it fast, wave it to take us back to the past.'

Pull out of the large bag, the second identical bag containing the 'horse' articles. The children must guess what this bag will contain; remind them to think back to the rhyme. Choose a child in turn to take out one article at a time, discussing what it is and how it may be used. Once all the articles have been revealed, relate these to those seen earlier, describing how they link together to show that horses were used for travelling in the past instead of cars. Contrast the items, for example car – horse, petrol pump – hay, tyre – horseshoe to show what has changed.

Discussion
Talk to the children about the differences between these two forms of transport. Do you think Humpty Dumpty lived now or a long time ago? Where are cars kept? Where would horses have been kept? How do you fix a puncture? How were horseshoes fixed? What types of roads did horses travel on?

For younger children
Introduce the activity in the same way but reinforce the idea by showing the children pictures of transport long ago and now.

For older children
Encourage the children to think about the types of horses used in the past and the different ways in which they were used (farms, mines, transporting goods, coaches).

Follow-up activities
▲ Consider the changes that have taken place in cars (the variety, the colours, the shape, the use, the number).
▲ Consider the changes that have taken place with roads to accommodate the growth of cars (motorways, dual carriageways, street lights, road markings).
▲ Construct a survey to discover whether grandparents and great grandparents had a car and if so what colour it was.

Eggsperiences

Objective
Geography – to find out about the local area and to think about the environment.

Group size
Small groups.

What you need
Telescope or binoculars, large piece of plain fabric, wooden block, brown paint, low table, paper, card, drawing and writing materials.

Preparation
Use the wooden block and paint to print a brick wall on the large piece of fabric. When dry, drape this over a low table as a wall.

What to do
Explain to the children that Humpty Dumpty has been sitting on his wall using his telescope to look about and see what it is like where he lives. Ask the children in turn to sit on the 'wall' and use the telescope to see if they can spot their house. Tell them to pretend that they can and ask them to describe it in detail, along with the surrounding area.

Repeat this process, asking the children to locate a local area they would like to visit. Encourage the children to say why they like going to this place. What do they like or dislike about it? What would they change?

Following this, the children should draw or write about where they like to visit. Compile their work into a large book called 'Our Local Area.'

Discussion
Talk to the children about features of the local area. Where is your favourite place to visit? Where is your least favourite place to visit? How could you make it better – would you add something or take something away?

For younger children
Encourage younger children to learn their home address. Make luggage labels to attach to a Humpty Dumpty or display on a wall.

For older children
Provide opportunities for the children to compare the local area with another locality with differing characteristics.

Follow-up activities
▲ Discuss with the children the possible addresses for where Humpty Dumpty, the king or his men may live.
▲ Make a plan of what attractions you would like in your local area.

79

Starting with rhyme
Nursery rhyme activities

Eggstravaganza

Objective
Art – to explore collage, printing and painting.

Group size
Small groups.

What you need
Large pieces of card, smaller pieces of card, paper, sponges, wooden blocks, paint, selection of fabrics, crêpe paper, tissue paper, glue, scissors, drawing and colouring materials.

Preparation
Prepare the paint ready for the children to print, cover the work surface.

What to do
Explain to the children that they are to make a large picture of Humpty Dumpty, by working on different parts.

Create the background to the scene by asking the children to sponge print a blue sky and green grass. They can add blades of grass using strips of green tissue paper. Tell them to cut out a golden sun and stick this in the sky.

Make a wall by directing the children to cut out brick shapes which can be stuck onto the background in rows.

Choose a child to draw an outline of Humpty Dumpty onto coloured paper and encourage the other children to add facial

features, arms, legs and a belt. Stick Humpty Dumpty onto his wall.

Once the large picture is complete encourage the children to each make their own smaller individual pictures.

Discussion
Talk to the children about the picture and its features. Is the sky always blue? Is the grass always green? What other shades of colour could you have? Discuss what else the children could add to their picture (flowers, trees) and ask what shape and colours these would be.

For younger children
Encourage the children to make their individual pictures using pre-cut shapes and by printing Humpty Dumpty's wall using a small brick dipped in paint.

For older children
Challenge the children to mix different shades with the paint for the sky and grass. Encourage them to add more detail to their individual pictures by adding clouds, flowers and trees.

Follow-up activities
▲ Make a collage of horses and soldiers to add to the picture.
▲ Illustrate the whole nursery rhyme by creating a different picture to accompany each scene.
▲ Make collage books of Humpty Dumpty by collaging different scenes and displaying the appropriate text with the picture.

Ding, dong, wall

Objective
Music – to experience the musical elements of timbre, structure and texture.

Group size
Small groups.

What you need
Selection of instruments (wood blocks, cymbals, drums, tambourine, maracas), paper, writing and drawing materials.

Preparation
Make a large copy of the Humpty Dumpty rhyme. Photocopy several small pictures of the instruments to be used.

What to do
Display the large copy of the nursery rhyme and read Humpty Dumpty together. Look at the instruments together and choose each child in turn to play one. As each instrument is played encourage the children to listen carefully and discuss which part of the nursery rhyme it accompanies best (such as using cymbals for when Humpty had a great fall; and using wood blocks for when the horses arrive).

Once the instruments have been allocated to a part of the nursery rhyme, say the rhyme together adding the correct instruments at the appropriate time.

To demonstrate this as a pattern/score, cut and stick the pictures of the instruments onto paper, and point to the appropriate picture as the children play and sing.

Discussion
Discuss with the children: When would we play an instrument loud and when should we play one quietly? Which instruments do we shake? Which instruments do we tap? Are there any instruments we shake and tap? How can we play a drum quietly? What do quiet instruments make us think of?

For younger children
Prepare a sheet for the children to follow with the symbols on and limit the number of instruments.

For older children
Encourage the children to make their own patterns to play with their friends.

Follow-up activities
▲ Give the children a selection of familiar patterns to perform and to guess what the tune is.
▲ Introduce some simple tunes using the chime bars.
▲ Make your own patterns and tunes to familiar nursery rhymes or poems.

Egg roll

Objective
PE – to develop skills in sending, receiving and travelling with a variety of balls.

Group size
Small or large groups.

What you need
Different sized balls (table tennis, small airflow, tennis, sponge and large balls), ropes and a tambourine.

Preparation
Discuss with the children the need to listen to and act on instructions. Stress the importance of safety when using a confined space, and position the apparatus in the corners for the children to gain easy access.

What to do
Warm-up
On command ask the children to gallop like the king's horses, or march like the king's men in and out of the space. Shout commands or hit the tambourine as a signal for change.

Lay ropes at a variety of angles, as the children march to the end of the rope, they have to turn and march to the next rope.

Main activity
Let the children choose a ball and return to their space keeping the ball still. Explain to the children that they must pretend their ball is an egg like Humpty Dumpty. They must try not to drop their balls as they practise throwing them into the air and catching them.

After an initial practice the children may choose a different sized ball.

Ask the children to find a partner. After one child in the pair has returned their ball, encourage the children to practise throwing and catching to each other.

Challenge the children to discover as many ways as possible to send the ball to their partner, for example, throwing with one hand, over their head, chest passes, overarm, underarm, rolling and bouncing.

To develop the children's skills further, increase the throwing distance by encouraging them to move away from their partner, put one hand behind their back, or use a smaller ball.
Cool down
Choose pairs of children to demonstrate their skills to the rest of the group. After returning the apparatus, ask the children to lie down, pretending to be a broken Humpty Dumpty and relax all their muscles.

Discussion
Talk to the children about the importance of keeping healthy and fit. What happens to your heart and blood when you exercise? Does your heartbeat feel different when you start compared to when you finish? When does it beat the fastest? When it is beating fast what is happening to your blood? What happens when you get hot from exercising? What would happen if you did not warm up or cool down?

For younger children
Build up the children's skills more gradually, focusing on one aspect per session. Begin by using large sponge balls or hedgehog balls.

For older children
Ask the children to practise their throwing and catching skills whilst moving around the space. Introduce the children to simple fielding skills.

Follow-up activities
▲ Use the new skills in invasion (attacking and defending) and target games.
▲ Develop your own games, making up your own rules.
▲ Practise aiming skills by using hoops, cones or ropes for target practice.

Eggstra nice

Objective
RE – to foster positive attitudes towards each other.

Group size
Large or small groups.

What you need
Pre-cut paper bricks, pictures of Humpty Dumpty in sequence, writing and drawing materials.

Preparation
Draw a sequential set of Humpty Dumpty pictures.

What to do
Look at the pictures of Humpty Dumpty. Discuss with the children who is in the picture and ask how they think Humpty Dumpty feels about sitting by himself. Relate this to how they feel when they are by themselves. Ask them to suggest ways they can help each other when they have these kinds of feelings.

Consider the next picture of Humpty Dumpty falling off the wall, repeat the same process, asking the children what they are thinking and how they feel.

Proceed with the next picture of the king's men helping Humpty Dumpty and talk about how they helped him feel better.

Challenge the children to help somebody during the day. When they have been helpful suggest that they could write or draw on a brick to show what they have done. Explain that you will build a wall with their bricks to make a wall of kindness. Ask them to see how tall they can make the wall, over a set period of time.

Discussion
As this activity is discussion-based ensure all the children participate and respect each other's feelings. Much of the discussion will focus on their own thoughts and feelings and how to help others.

For younger children
Establish set tasks or activities for the children to complete in order to achieve bricks for the wall, for example by inviting a new friend to play.

For older children
Divide the children into two groups and let the groups compete to see who can build the highest wall, over a set period.

Follow-up activities
▲ Read or tell stories relating to feelings and emotions, including loneliness, fear and hurt.
▲ Write stories or poems based around the central theme of loneliness or fear.
▲ Demonstrate different feelings and emotions using facial expressions.

Transport then and now

What you need
Pictures of different forms of transport past and present, paper, colouring and writing materials, paint, nail brush, tissue paper, glue, blocks to print, sponges, gummed paper, wool, ribbon and corrugated card.

Preparation
Cover the work surface and make the resources available. Separate the display board horizontally into two, labelled: 'Travel in the past' and 'Travel in the present'.

What to do
The children should work in groups on different aspects of the display.

To create a three-dimensional effect, attach loops of card onto the back of appropriate objects before stapling to wall.

Section One – 'In the past'
Cobble stones: print a cobbled pathway with blocks and grey paint. Print along the centre and outline the path in black.

Trees: mix brown paint with glue. Drag a nail brush through to give a bark effect. Scrunch up green tissue paper for leaves

Horses: paint an outline of several horses, mix brown paint with glue to paint them.

Use brown wool for a mane and tail.

Carts: paint different types of carts. Cut out and attach to the horses with ribbon/wool.

People: paint people in different positions to add to the display.

Section Two – 'In the present'
Background: sponge print the road black, add white lines as road markings. Sponge print a blue sky.

Pavement: create a pavement by taking rubbings from the pavement or carpet tiles.

Houses: paint a selection of houses, paying attention to numbers and colours.

Train track and trains: use corrugated card, as the train track. Paint a variety of carriages, attach wheels and secure to the track.

Vehicles: paint various vehicles for the road.

Discussion
Talk about the differences between the two sections of the display. Are there houses in both displays? What are the roads like?

Follow-up activities
▲ Discover and display the differences between other areas (houses, shops).

▲ Display aspects of your locality and record the changes over time.

Wall of kindness

What you need
Paint, sponges, large blocks to print bricks, aprons, paper, card, writing and colouring materials, collage materials, pre-cut brick shaped paper.

Preparation
Cover the work surface. Separate the display board into three.

What to do
The children should work in groups to complete the display. When the children complete a 'kind deed' they can draw or write it on a pre-cut brick shape and stick it on the appropriate section of the display.

Background
Sponge print paper blue and green to give the effect of sky and grass.

Section 1
Print a wall using wooden bricks and paint. Draw and collage Humpty Dumpty using either a selection of fabrics or papers, make concertina arms and legs. Sit Humpty Dumpty on the wall. Encourage the children to think of appropriate words to display around the picture to describe Humpty: lonely, quiet, sad, unhappy and so on.

Section 2
Print a wall as in Section 1. Draw and collage a sad Humpty Dumpty, and then cut him in half to leave jagged edges and attach him at the bottom of the wall. Display some appropriate words around the picture: hurt, broken, sore, upset and so on.

Section 3
Print a third wall as described. Collage a Humpty Dumpty complete with a bandaged stomach! Children can draw and collage the king's men and horses and place these close to Humpty Dumpty in front of the wall. Write some words to describe the scene: better, help, happy, fixed, mended.

Discussion
Talk about times when the children feel the same way as Humpty does in the different pictures. How can we help our friends be happy? How can we look after our friends? How can we help someone who is sad? How can we help them feel better?

Follow-up activities
▲ Make books of 'kind deeds' and position these near to the display.
▲ Ask the children to suggest a series of possible 'kind deeds' and record these onto a pathway leading up to the walls, uncovering one of the kind deeds per day for them to try and complete.

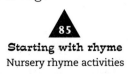

Pancakes

Group size
Small groups.

What you need.
200g plain flour, ¼ teaspoon sugar, ¼ teaspoon salt, 2 eggs, half-litre milk, oil for frying, lemon, syrup, jam, sugar, honey, frying pan, cooker, electric whisk, bowl, small dish, sieve, fish slice, plate and ladle. Photocopiable page 96.

Preparation
Photocopy page 96 for each child. Make the batter mixture by sieving the flour, sugar and salt into a bowl. Make a well in the centre, add the broken eggs and 100ml of milk, stir gradually, working in the flour, adding more milk as required. Whisk well, add the remaining milk, cover and leave to stand for a while.

What to do
Whilst the batter is standing, discuss with the children the differences in the ingredients used, how they have changed from a powder to a liquid and the heating process involved to make the mixture into pancakes.

Ensure the children are aware of the dangers related to the hot pan, cooker and cooked pancakes and keep them well away from the cooking area.

Show the children the different fillings, explaining that all the fillings will be used for them to taste.

Heat oil in a frying pan, pouring the excess into a small dish. Ladle a spoonful of mixture into the hot frying pan, making sure the base of the pan is evenly covered with mixture. Move the frying pan over the heat to free the mixture from the sides. When the pancake is set and light brown, toss or turn with a fish slice. When cooked turn onto a plate, add a filling, roll and cut into slices for the children to taste.

Repeat this process several times to ensure all the fillings have been used.

Afterwards, invite the children to find out what the most popular filling was by asking their friends, and completing photocopiable page 96.

Discussion
Relate the breaking of the eggs into the flour with Humpty Dumpty and how he looked when he was broken. Discuss the fillings for the pancakes. What is your favourite filling? What is your least favourite filling? Do all pancake fillings have to be sweet?

Follow-up activities
▲ Think of a 'new pancake filling'.
▲ Find out which pancake filling was the most popular on the graph.
▲ Record the process and ingredients used to make the pancakes using pictures.

Take your pick

▲ Draw some arrows to match the food.

Stop and shop

▲ Match the food to the shops.

Reach the clock

▲ Draw the path for the mouse to reach the clock, following the numbers.

Tick, tock, tick, tock

▲ Colour, cut and stick these pictures in order.

All in pieces

▲ Colour, cut and stick these pictures in order.

▲ Match the sentences to the pictures.

Jack and Jill went up the hill	Jack fell down and broke his crown,
and Jill came tumbling after.	to fetch a pail of water.

▲ 91
Starting with rhyme
Nursery rhyme activities

photocopiable
▶ **activities** ◀

Up the hill

▲ Draw a taller hill for Jack and Jill to climb.

▲ Now draw a smaller one.

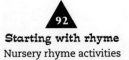

A special invitation

▲ Cut and fold along the petals.

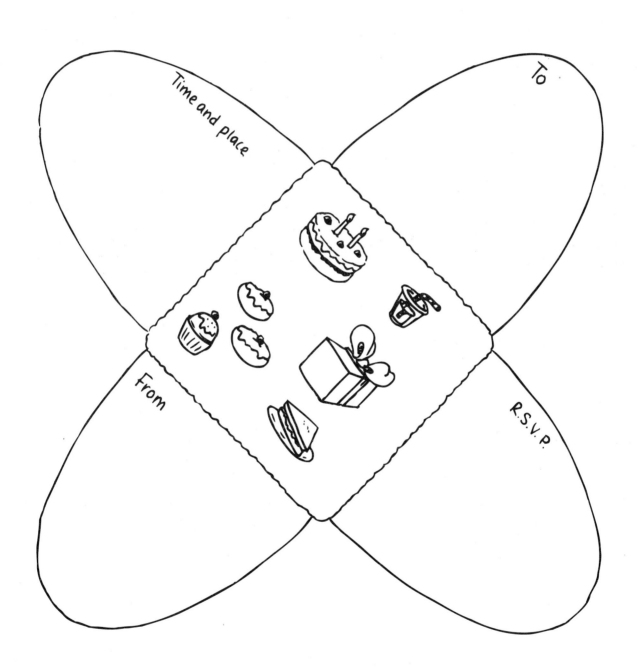

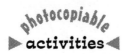

Musical Mary

photocopiable ►activities◄

Rescuing Humpty

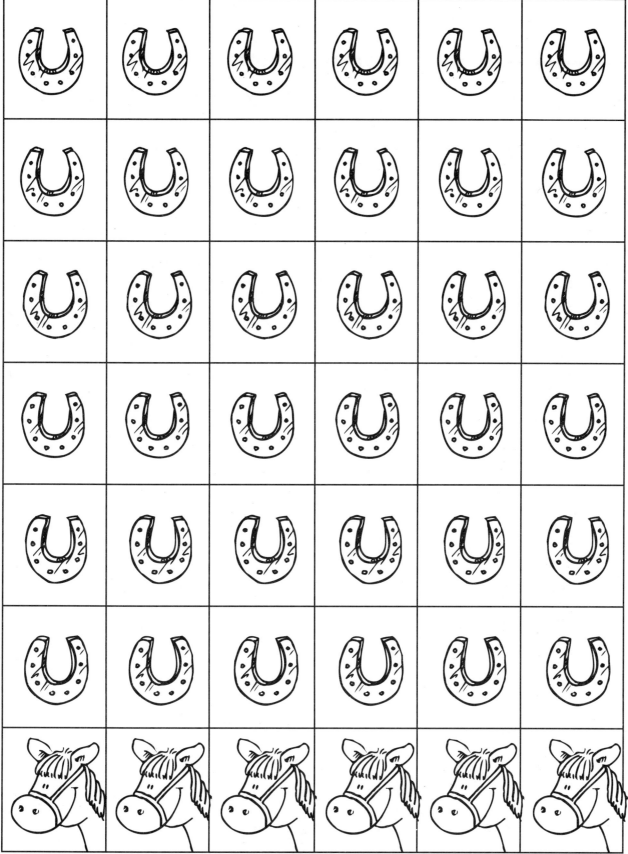

95
Starting with rhyme
Nursery rhyme activities

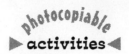

Pancake treats

▲ Find out what pancake fillings your friends like.

▲ Write their names on this chart.

lemon	jam	syrup	sugar	honey